THE
PASTOR'S
PEN

Volume I

Nuggets for Life and Leading
from a Pastor's Perspective

Tim S. Estes

First Printing: 2020

Tim S. Estes
P. O. Box 475
Siloam Springs, AR 72761

tim@nlcss.com

Scripture quotations taken from The Holy Bible, New International Version NIV
Copyright 1973, 1978, 1984, 2011 by Biblica, Inc.
Used by permission. All rights reserved worldwide.

Also used:
Scripture quotations taken from the New American Standard Bible (NASB)
Copyright 1960, 1962, 1963, 1968, 1971, 1972, 1973, 1975, 1977, 1995 by the Lockman Foundation
Used by permission. www.Lockman.org

Also used:
Scripture quotations from The Authorized (King James) Version.
Rights in the Authorized Version in the United Kingdom are vested in the Crown. Reproduced by permission of the Crown's patentee, Cambridge University Press.

In Memory

of

Jan Mullikin

TABLE OF CONTENTS

PREFACE

Each Monday the article was due for the mid-week edition of the paper. The deadline for weekly publication demanded timely transmission of documents, while the limited print-space required concise thoughts and succinct writing.

For a decade the author hit the 'send' button and thousands of people became the recipients of inspirational/biblical thoughts pertaining to a variety of topics from leading and learning, to values and virtues. Each chapter in this book represents a different article and is duplicated from its original writing.

In the office of the local paper, The Herald Leader, the author found many wonderful friendships. One especially stands out. Her name was Jan. Jan Mullikin was an editor, a gospel singer, a wife and mother, a writer and most of all…a Christian friend. Her earthly work is now ended and this book is dedicated to the memory of her many contributions to our community, and to me as a friend.

You may find humor in some of the comments that will obviously reflect the time in which they were written. However, the principles within the stories will always stand the test of time. Hopefully, you will find enjoyment, inspiration and nuggets of truth for your life, as you read.

I gratefully acknowledge my family and wife, Tricia, who was my first-line editor. They bless my life with an enormity no pen could ever describe. I am grateful to God for His grace, … to my family for their love,...and to you the reader for your investment.

Please enjoy!

Tim S. Estes

1

YOU CAN LIVE ON BUTTER AND HONEY

Our figure-conscious society has a diet to fit everyone. In
fact, dieting has become a fad. From Slim-Fast to garlic
pills, we are looking for a way to get fit. I do not know if
garlic helps you lose weight, but it makes you look good
from a distance. In Isaiah 7:15 there is a diet mentioned
that, when applied to our lives, is sure to help us all.

Notice Isaiah's prophetic writing concerning the Messiah,
Jesus Christ: "…and shall call His name Emmanuel.
Butter and honey shall He eat that He may know to refuse
the evil and choose the good."

Why would God take the time and space to notify you and I
of Christ's diet? The obvious answer is to demonstrate He
would be reared as a common man. If God in flesh had
been sheltered in a palace, preserved from temptation and
suffering, we would not relate to Him. However, He was
tempted like we are, was a man of like passions and had the
rough edges of His earthly nature hewn in a common
carpenter's shop. Instead of steak and lobster served on a
silver platter, Jesus was more familiar with beans and
cornbread, with 'butter and honey.'

Butter and honey represent a proper balance to living.
Those of you reading this who are 50 years old and above,
know that butter did not always come in plastic containers.

On the family farm, the cream was separated from the milk, placed in a churn and someone had to go to work.
That's right. If you are going to have butter you are going to have to use some elbow grease. Butter represents our efforts, ethics, disciplines and honor. Butter is the part of living that assists our ability to refuse evil. The best defense against evil is to busy oneself doing right things.

What about the honey? Honey is a delicacy almost everyone enjoys. The best part about the honey is you and I haven't the ability to make a drop of it. Honey is made by the busy bee who, upon ascertaining nectar from flowers, uses his body as a machine to produce honey. Honey is a free benefit we do not have to work for. Honey represents the blessings of God daily given to each of us. They are undeserved and often unexpected.

The Psalmist noted the Lord daily loads us with benefits. I believe our Heavenly Father enjoys blessing you and me. Just as you enjoy seeing your children healthy and happy, so God derives pleasure from seeing you smile. This portion is decided by your choice. You must choose to see and enjoy the good that is around you.

Here is the key to this healthy diet. There must be a balance of both ingredients in order to live with spiritual health. When it is time to employ your skills, do it with all of your might. Yet, we must remember, "All work and no play makes Jack a dull boy." If you are overboard on the disciplines – are a workaholic – lighten up and look up to see there is a good deal of honey and sweetness you have been missing. On the other hand, if your life is consumed with nothing but thrill seeking, your sweet tooth is probably aching. Many times those who complain of never getting a break in life are those who have become "honey junkies" and usually have lost their grip on the handle of the butter churn.

If you need further proof of this theory, try this. Take a homemade roll out of the oven. While it is still hot, spread some sure-enough cow butter on it. Just as the butter melts, drip some mild honey on top and then sample it. You will be convinced! This combination was made in heaven. It is a diet we can all live with!

2

EVERYONE ENJOYS THE SONG OF THE BROOK

Growing up on the banks of the Illinois River, I developed a keen appreciation for rivers and streams. It has been my privilege to wade crystal clear streams while fishing for trout high in the mountains of Colorado and Quebec. In each case, the enjoyment of both seeing and hearing the water was truly relaxing. Anytime I have camped near a creek, it was truly wonderful sleeping to the song of the brook. This tranquil trickling sound is so relaxing, they now have mini-water falls to place in homes so as to imitate the sound of running water.

Have you ever stopped to think what gives the brook its song? What creates the sound of gurgling, rushing water making music for our ears and souls? It is obviously the rocks that produce the sound in the stream. Were it not for the rocks and boulders standing in opposition to the running water the brook would run still and silent. Remove the opposition and you eliminate the song.

Now, think of your life. Got boulders? Do you have some rocks jutting their ugly, opposing heads above otherwise tranquil waters of your soul? Sure you do. We all do! The lists of opponents are too numerous to mention and yet they all have one thing in common. They help bring music to the brook.

Notice the words of Jeremiah in Lamentations 1:16, "For these things I weep…" Most of the 'rocks' of life can be categorized as one of "these things." Upon further study I noted there is a complete list in many concordances under the heading of 'these things.' 'These things' might be an illness that refuses to go away. To another, loneliness could be the boulder of their life. Family issues or financial problems certainly can fall under the same heading.

The great Apostle Paul, in his letter to the church at Rome (Romans 8:31) gave tremendous wisdom concerning our trials. "What shall we then say to these things?" he wrote. "If God be for us who can be against us?" This is truly the point of the entire issue at hand. It really does not matter what rises up to oppose your life. Nothing will stop the river from running. Rocks of temptation, trial, persecution or ill health cannot stop your Christian walk. These boulders only cause the water to fight harder and find a way over, under or around, and in doing so, create the sound of sweet music the whole world will enjoy.

Remember the shepherd boy, David? When he was about to face the giant on the battlefield, he made a trip down to the brook. Imagine him sitting on the bank with his bare feet in the water enjoying the sunshine and listening to the water. The Bible makes distinct mention of the stones David selected as ammo for his sling. There were 'five smooth stones.' Notice, they were 'smooth' stones. Stones that one day had risen up against the current. Stones that had been worn away, eroded and ultimately shaped by the inexorable flow of water. They must have preached a message of hope to the little warrior. "You can defeat your enemy!" "You can overcome!" "No weapon formed against you will prosper!"

A similar message was given to the old prophet Elijah. Wearied from the work, he was instructed by God to hide beside the brook Cherith (I Kings 17). Recall with me that God told the prophet he would be fed daily by a raven and that he should get his water from the brook. I have to believe God sent him to the brook to teach him a lesson. Each time Elijah was thirsty he put his face close to the water and listened to the music. The tune of the tide and the chorus of the creek sang a song of sweet victory. "The water always wins!"

If you are facing a severe difficulty, become aware of the beautiful music your life produces as you triumph over each day. If God be for you...nothing can stop you! That is the song of the brook...and everyone enjoys the sound!

3

FAITH HAS A FIRST COUSIN

Think through your mental catalog of Bible characters. See if you recognize the names…Shammua, Shaphat, Igal, Palti, Gaddiel, Gaddi, Ammiel, Sethur, Nahbi, Geuel. Having trouble? Me too! Try these names…Joshua and Caleb, do you recognize them? Of course we do! The reason we did not know the first group of names is basically because they are unimportant. They are unimportant because they were ten of twelve spies that came back with an evil report from the land of Canaan (Numbers 13). Nobody cares to remember the faithless and fearful, but we all love to recall those who were filled with faith and the spirit of godly adventure. Joshua and Caleb's names are justly preserved for the ages.

Faith has a first cousin. It is called Courage. Faith is our trust in God and belief that He will provide, protect and meet whatever need we have. Courage is acting on the premise of our foundational belief. Faith is the springboard and courage is the will to jump from it. Faith provoked the three Hebrew children to say, "Our God is well able to deliver us," but it took courage to act on that faith and willfully go into the fiery furnace. A New York City firefighter, Michael Crowell, defined it well. "Courage is when you're afraid but you do it anyway."

Several generations ago, during a desert war in the Middle East, a spy was captured and sentenced to death by a general of the Persian army. The general, a man of intelligence and compassion, had adopted an unusual custom in such cases. He permitted the condemned person to make a choice. The prisoner could either face a firing squad or pass through the Black Door. As the moment of the execution drew near, the general ordered the spy to be brought before him for a short, final interview and to gain an answer to the query: "What shall it be? The firing squad or the Black Door?"

This was not an easy decision, but soon the prisoner made it known that he much preferred the firing squad to the unknown horrors that might await him behind the ominous and mysterious door. Moments later, a volley of gunshots announced the grim sentence had been fulfilled.

The general staring at his boots, turned to his aide and said, "You see how it is with men; they will always prefer the known to the unknown. It is the characteristic of people to be afraid of the undefined."

"What lies behind the Black Door?" asked the aide.

"Freedom," replied the general, "and I've known only a few brave enough to take it."

Are you thinking about kicking an old habit, attempting to resolve a marital fray, giving more time and finances to your church, changing jobs to allow more time for your children, or rededicating your life to God? Be courageous and do it! Do not be condemned to the ignoble mass of humanity who will forever be chronicled in the anonymity of average oblivion. Become a Joshua or a Caleb. Success depends not only on what you believe, but also what you do about what you believe. Introduce yourself to faith's first cousin.

4

WHEN IT RAINS, IT POURS

I recall singing a little song as a child that went something like this, "Rain, rain go away, come again another day…" This was especially appropriate when waking up to the sound of thunder on a day planned with fun activities. If you have children around, you may have heard this song the past few weeks.

While recently studying Christ's Sermon on the Mount, I gave some thought to our Lord's words in Matthew 5:45. "For He makes His sun to rise on the evil and on the good, and sends rain on the just and on the unjust." From this passage we are made to know the equality of God. He affords the opportunity of mercy to every man, deserving or not. He blesses each of us with some 'common ground' blessing. The same sun warming the back of the banker, also warms the back of the bank robber. The very same rain that grows flowers for the judge, grows opiates for the crook.

Most often, in this text, rain is spoken of metaphorically as trouble. It is correct to interpret as such. Rain may also be noted as blessing. To the family stranded by a flood on their rooftop, rain definitely is a nemesis. Yet, to a drought-stricken farmer whose livelihood depends on rain, every drop is precious.

This brings us to the application. We have trouble understanding the ways of God with our finite, human reasoning. When rain comes in the form of trouble, it seems fair to dump it on the bad guys and highly unfair that the Christian should have to endure it. On the other hand, when rain is in the form of blessing our minds see another inequity. We applaud when a 'good guy' is blessed. That is the way it is supposed to be! When a cheater gets the promotion on the job or a lazy bum inherits a million dollars, we slam our fist on the table and demand to know what is going on! It is difficult to watch an avowed, hardened criminal go unpunished or receive an early parole. It is equally difficult to watch a senior citizen, after working hard all of their lives, struggle to pay for medical bills, food and other necessities on limited income. It just is not fair!

Scrolling through the list of notable Bible characters, few are exempt from extreme trials and circumstances. Jacob suffered a severe injury early in life. Job found himself in an all-encompassing bankruptcy. David was innocently targeted for an assassination. John was imprisoned. Paul was beaten and shipwrecked. Where is the fair play in all of this? After all, these were great men of God! I am not saying we are destined for much trial when we become a Christian, but please be aware we are not exempt from it either. I Peter 5:9 says, "The same afflictions are accomplished in your brethren that are in the world." The beautiful part is God uses these difficulties to make us better. Shakespeare said, "In sickness, let me not so much say, Am I getting better of my pain; but am I getting better for it."

I have some great news for you. The final chapter has not been written. God's eternal scales of equality will be balanced at the judgment. "So then every one of us shall give account of himself to God." (Romans 14:12) Sneers of the unrighteous will turn to mourning, while the believer who may have wept through the night, will face the dawn with a smile. Do not curse the rain, get an umbrella! May the Lord bless you this week!

5

THE LORD IS MY SHEPHERD

When David wrote the 23rd Psalm, he was writing from the perspective of a shepherd in Palestine. In the context of his custom, shepherding was and is different than we know of in our country. A closer look at the meaning can make this blessed old psalm come alive.

THE LORD IS MY SHEPHERD:
From the beginning of this chapter we establish the priority of relationship. A sheep is one of the most dependent of animals. A sheep has no claws, no fangs, nor a shell to crawl into. The existence of a sheep depends upon the defense of the shepherd. Jesus used this analysis in Matthew 10:16, when He said to His disciples, "Behold I send you out as sheep among wolves." This must not be interpreted as a set up for failure. To the contrary, it is a lesson of our total dependence upon God, the Good Shepherd. In the Middle East, shepherds often brought several different flocks of sheep to the same barn, or fold, for the night. When morning came, the flocks were separated by the voice of the shepherd. One shepherd would step to the door of the barn and call for his sheep. The sheep that belonged to him would perk up their ears and follow him out of the barn. Likely it is this custom to which Jesus referred when He said, "My sheep know My voice." (See John 10:3-4)

HE MAKETH ME LIE DOWN IN GREEN PASTURES:
In a land where plentiful pastures were scarce, a shepherd
had to remain on the move to keep his sheep satisfied.
Also, when a sheep grazes, it will eat the grass down to the
root and destroy the pasture. Shepherds continually rotated
to new pastures to prevent overgrazing. The Lord always
provides daily bread and spiritual nourishment in both
quality and quantity. His sheep never have to worry about
provision. If we follow Him, we will always lie down in
green pastures.

Being animals of prey, sheep are very nervous. They have
many enemies in the wild such as the coyote, bear, wolf
and lion. A sheep that is afraid will scarcely lie down.
Only when the sheep senses the safety of the shepherd's
presence will it lie down for rest. In Jesus we can find a
place of refuge and safety.

HE LEADETH ME BESIDE THE STILL WATERS:
Knowing the nature of sheep, David wrote this verse.
Sheep are not comfortable drinking from a bubbling
stream. The noise and the rapids make them afraid. Since
our Shepherd knows all about us, He always provides the
best for us. Our Shepherd leads us to still, quiet, reflective
waters where we feel comfortable and can be refreshed.

THOUGH I WALK THROUGH THE VALLEY OF THE
SHADOW OF DEATH I WILL FEAR NO EVIL:
In Palestine, they say there is an actual place called the
"Valley of the Shadow of Death." This valley is known for
its rough and treacherous slopes that can be especially

dangerous if a sheep wanders away from the flock. In life we all pass through this valley as well, either through the loss of a loved one or as we face death ourselves. There is no greater comfort than to know Jesus will take the sting of death away. We do not have to fear this valley because our Shepherd does not send us through it alone. He walks with us!

THY ROD AND THY STAFF THEY COMFORT ME: The shepherd's staff was a common tool of the trade. Basically, it was a long stick with a crook or curve at the top. The straight portion of the tool was the rod and the curved end was the staff. You may have seen an artist's rendering of a shepherd extending his staff to a lamb which had fallen from a rocky ledge. When you and I fall, it is comforting to feel the staff of our Shepherd hook us gently and lift us from certain death.

On the other hand, the comfort of the rod must be seen in the big picture. Like human beings, there are sheep that constantly endanger themselves by leaving the flock. A wayward sheep is vulnerable to getting lost, or worse, being killed by a predator. If this practice becomes a habit, a shepherd might take his rod and break a leg of the wayward sheep. As cruel as this may sound, the shepherd is actually doing the little sheep a favor. By inflicting this pain, it creates a realization of its vulnerability and therefore causes the sheep to stay close to the shepherd. God knows we sometimes need the touch of the rod in order to stay close to Him.

At the end of the day, when the flock makes it to the barn or shelter, the shepherd stands at the door and causes each sheep to enter the barn by passing under the rod. (See Ezekiel. 20:37) This is the way the shepherd counts his sheep and individually checks their health. No wonder the psalmist wrote of the comfort found in the rod and staff.

When the day is complete and all sheep accounted for, the shepherd lays down across the door of the sheep fold. He protects and preserves the life of his flock with his own life. Want to be well fed, cared for and loved? Get to know the Chief Shepherd, Jesus Christ. He laid down His life for you. He wants you in His fold.

6

GOD HAS A PLAN FOR EACH TO FOLLOW

Two friends of mine are brothers. They are both successful, both very talented and both are competitive. One of the brothers bought a game of chess and began to play with it, learning the movements of the chess pieces and developing a strategy. One day this man's brother came by. Upon seeing the chess board he decided to try his hand at it. In just a few minutes the game was over. The words of the brother who lost hold a lesson for life. He said, "I knew I had lost when I saw that I was just moving chess pieces and he had a plan."

God doesn't want you and me to wander through life hopeless and helpless. A trial and error existence would be miserable. Someone said, "Learn from the mistakes of others, you'll never live long enough to make them all yourself." We must look to the Bible, the living Word of God, as our roadmap.

Throughout the Bible, God has worked with meticulous plans. Noah was given specific plans for success which he followed perfectly. He built the ark to the exact specifications God told him to build. Plans for the tabernacle and its furnishings were given to Moses with the most intricate detail. Prophets would forewarn men of coming perils and give perfect details under the inspiration of God.

In Acts 9 we read of Saul's conversion. A man named Ananias was told by God to go to a town, to a certain street and inquire of a man he had never met, dwelling at a specific house. Talk about planning! Scripture gives many illustrations of those who failed to follow God's plan and how they suffered for it. Moses was a great leader and did many wonderful things, however, he was not privileged to enter the Promised Land because he failed to speak to the rock as he was instructed. Instead, he smote the rock and learned how vitally important it was to follow God's plan.

Remember Lot's wife? She is the one immortalized as a pillar of salt. Her life is a memorial to failure, not because she didn't have a way of escape, but simply because she did not completely follow God's plan. God has a plan for you and me. He went to Calvary to provide a way for all men to be saved. It behooves everyone to follow His footsteps and His plan. In Luke 24:45-49, prior to Christ's ascension, He left humanity with a reminder of salvation's plan. Jesus spoke of His death, burial and resurrection. Jesus applied this gospel to us by saying, "…that repentance (death), and remission of sins (burial, baptism) should be preached in His Name…and I send the promise of the Father upon you (resurrection, Spirit infilling)." This is the gospel plan for everyone!

Life is not a game. It is a reality! I do not want to merely shuffle days and relationships as pawns on the board. I'd rather use a strategy – His strategy. Doing so will make us winners every time!

7

HAVE YOU DISCOVERED GOD'S RESERVE?

Many summer days of my childhood were spent riding a yellow Honda Trail 90 motorcycle. It was great fun! Even though I was so small I could hardly hold it up, I felt like the world was mine sitting atop that thing. I learned to peel out, sling mud and ramp both wheels into the air (no wonder my mom was worried). One thing that took some time to learn was keeping an eye on the gas gauge. Becoming engrossed in the fun, it was easy to forget a most important thing – the fuel. More than one time I recall bringing my motorbike home on the energy of yours truly. It was no fun pushing a machine twice my own weight. Running out of gas was the pits!

Soon I was shown one of the neatest features ever seen. Regrettably, I had pushed my bike home several times before it was discovered. Beneath the seat, out of sight to the untrained eye, was a little switch known as the 'reserve switch.' If and when one ran out of fuel, all one had to do was turn the switch to 'reserve' and the needle in the gas tank would drop down to allow the usage of the last drops of fuel. Usually this was more than enough to get you home. What an awesome and most helpful discovery!

May I tell you that there will be times in all of our lives when we reach our limits? Really! There will come a day when you find the end of the line either physically, emotionally, financially, relationally, spiritually or all of the above. I think you can relate.

What does a person do in such a case? It is a bad feeling to be a long way from home on a cold night and feel your spirit sputter. Such was the case of one of the great prophets of the Old Testament, Elijah. I love this story because it reminds you and me that the best among us can have difficult times. Remember Elijah was the man anointed to prophesy to Ahab concerning both the season of drought and the times of rain. Both prophecies came to pass.

Elijah was the man used as the medium for monumental miracles. A dead boy was brought back to life under Elijah's ministry! Not the least of his highlights was the showdown at high noon with the 'Baal boys.' That is, 450 prophets of Baal confronted Elijah to see whose God was real. Of course, when the dust had settled, Jehovah had answered by fire and Baal proved to be invalid.

You would think a man of this caliber would never have a bad day. You and I know people who, from our vantage point, have it all going for them. What you may not know are the inner struggles and hidden tears they keenly mask behind their pseudo-smile. Elijah had his bad times too. Jezebel sent word to the prophet of her intent to kill him within 24 hours. It just so happened the news arrived about the same time the fuel gauge began to flash "E." The prophet ran all day. He was scared! He was empty!

Envision him running until his sides hurt – until his clothes were sweat soaked. When he finally collapsed in a cave, he asked God to take his life. "It is enough; now, O Lord, take away my life," were his words. (I Kings 19:4)
Depression steals rational thoughts from the mind. Exhaustion erodes necessary fibers of the soul. In such a place the prophet began to explain to the Lord his condition. Paraphrasing, he said, "Lord, I have worked hard for you, tried to do my best and now I am the only one left in Israel who really cares."

Romans chapter 11 recounts God's response to the prophet: "I have reserved to myself 7,000 men, who have not bowed the knee to the image of Baal." God has reserves! When you think you are in the battle alone – when you feel out of spiritual fuel, God has some extra in the tank. He is a more-than-enough God. He did not bring you this far to leave you. He would not give you a dream without fulfilling it. His Word says, "My God shall supply all your needs according to His riches in glory."

Ask God to help you find the reserve switch for your own life. Once you locate it, use it to your benefit. There will be enough fuel to get you home! Have a great week!

8

DO YOU DARE TO DREAM?

Genesis 37 tells the well-known story of Joseph, Jacob's son. Joseph was hated by his brothers, first because their father had made him a beautiful coat of many colors. Joseph was the favorite of his father, being his eleventh son and "…the son of his old age." This, however, was not the only reason he was hated. Joseph was a dreamer, and for this he was hated more.

Joseph's dream, and the fact that he told it to his brothers, was the driving force behind their hatred. This is the dream as told by Joseph: "We were binding sheaves in the field, and my sheaf arose and stood upright; and, behold your sheaves stood round about, and made obeisance to my sheaf." For this, says Genesis 37:8, "…they hated him yet the more."

It is a true fact that most things are born in the realms of dreams before they ever become reality. My grandfather was never a wealthy man but he was a dreamer. Being a carpenter, he enjoyed dreaming of ways to remodel his home. Many times we would talk about fantasy homes he wanted to build. His theory remains in my mind when he would say, "Son, it doesn't cost to dream…and sometimes dreams come true." I cannot tell you how many homes Grandpa remodeled and changed drastically for the better. He lived his dreams!

Life has a way of robbing us of our ability to dream. The older we become, the more we accept where we are in life. Let me challenge you to dream again. Look around you and think of the things that could be better. Resurrect an old idea you had years ago. Bring back to life some of your ambition! The dream can serve as the seed which, in time, will develop and grow into a wonderful reality.

Let me warn you as you begin to dream, there will be those who will not understand, who will become jealous, who will discourage you and will ultimately be in favor of selling you out. May we call it the Joseph Syndrome. The higher you rise, the more you become a target of the negative, stuck-in-a-rut 'elder brothers.' I recently read a cartoon where two whitetail deer were standing in a field. One looked normal, the other had a large, orange circle, like a target, on his side. The caption underneath said, "Bummer of a birthmark!" So it is with the dreamer.

Let me encourage you to accept the challenge, get the big picture in view and keep on dreaming! It may not come to pass today nor tomorrow, but in time it will happen. Joseph, after much time and many difficulties, stepped from behind the magnificent curtains of Pharaoh's chambers. Kneeling before him were his brothers, the "sheaves" he had dreamt of many years before. If God puts the dream in your heart, He knows how to bring it to pass. Keep on dreaming! Dreamers change the world!

9

WHEN JESUS SAYS, "I FEEL YOUR PAIN," BELIEVE IT!

"Laugh and the world laughs with you, weep and you weep alone," the old proverb says. In the human sense there is an element of truth to the saying, but when it comes to our Heavenly Father, He will always laugh and cry with you. We are never alone.

The words, "I feel your pain" almost became a laughable cliché' from the lips of some politicians. It was a great slogan for making us think they genuinely cared for the needs of the public. Granted, some of them may truly care, yet I am sure many cared more about our votes than our pain.

In the Gospel of Mark chapter 5, there is an account of a woman with a severe blood disorder. She had dealt with a continual hemorrhage for 12 years. Her story is the story of an incurable disease. Doctors had been consulted. Perhaps the home remedies of the day had been tried and all to no avail. The Bible states she had suffered many things. Not only that, but she was now at the end of her finances. Verse 26 states, "…and she had spent all that she had and was not better but grew worse."

Pale, weak and very anemic, she made her way to Jesus using her last bit of strength to press through the crowd. At last, she collapsed at His feet while grasping for the hem of Christ's robe.

The notable thing about the story is the fact that Jesus felt this touch. His disciples marveled and even questioned Him. "Lord, you see this huge crowd around You. What do You mean by asking, 'Who touched my clothes?"

They were insinuating the obvious, "Of course your clothes have been touched." Yet, Jesus knew this touch was different, He felt the need of this woman. At last she had met the man who could both feel her pain and do something about it. He understood her like nobody else in the world could.

Hebrews 4:15 is one of my favorite scriptures. It reminds us of our Great High Priest, Jesus Christ, who is touched with the feelings of our pain and weaknesses, When Jesus says, "I feel your pain," believe it!

He knows you and me more intimately than we could possibly know ourselves. He made us! He knows our thoughts. He knew about this year and next year in your life and every moment you will ever live, long before you were ever conceived. More than knowing, He truly cares and will help you!

There may be someone reading this who may be battling a lengthy illness. Someone may be grieving from the loss of a friend or loved one. Others may be attempting to deal with difficult family matters.

Perhaps your pain is of a nature that you feel you can't share it with anyone. Rest assured somebody, the only One who can really do anything about everything, already knows – and He cares.

When Jesus feels your pain, He will make a remedy for it. In fact, the remedy has already been completed. Isaiah 53 declares, "…with His stripes, we are healed."

I conclude with the words of the old song we all love:

What a Friend we have in Jesus;
All our sins and grief to bear.
What a privilege to carry,
Everything to God in prayer.
Oh, what peace we often forfeit;
Oh, what needless pain we bear;
All because we do not carry,
Everything to God in prayer.

May the Lord bless you and heal you.

10

WHERE DID THE GOOD TIMES GO?

Most of the time, a goal of ministry is to attempt to curb the appetites of mankind away from carnality and turn them toward spiritual things. That is, things that please our flesh generally rob the fruit of the spirit from the tree of the soul. There are times however, when those on the opposite end of the spectrum must be addressed. Strange as it may seem, there are those who seldom smile, rarely take a break and become workaholics. We sometimes refer to them as being people who are so heavenly-minded they are of no earthly good.

While I could spend a good deal of time writing on the virtues of work ethic and the dangers of spending too much time and money on the pleasures of life, it is my desire to present a balanced approach to living for God. Being balanced means having some fun, taking a break and attempting to enjoy the days allotted on this earth.

Perhaps you are one of those giving, service-minded people who derive a good deal of pleasure from helping others. While this is ripe with merit, it also holds some inherent danger. If one is not careful, they can assist their fellowman to the neglect of their own spiritual and physical well-being. There are times when it is okay to do some things just for yourself without the feeling of guilt.

Obviously, if this is the routine and habit of each day of your life there may be a problem.

Notice the writing of Paul in his first letter to Timothy (6:17), "Charge them that are rich in this world, that they be not high-minded, nor trust in uncertain riches, but in the living God, who gives us richly all things to enjoy." Understand it is God who gave us all things to enjoy. God meant for us to live a life with an abundance of joy. He made us with the ability to laugh. He is not the cosmic killjoy! He is the God of all joy!

I must say that real enjoyment is that which comes from God. Most of the things we call pleasure are man-made substitutes for the authentic. Disneyland and Six Flags definitely have their limits of enjoyment, especially the older I get. One can ascertain only a certain amount of happiness from new things...boats, cars, houses, toys. These things all lose their luster with time. The things that bring lasting joy are from the Lord.

How long has it been since you enjoyed a picnic with your family or a friend? When was the last time you called up an old friend and shared a great conversation? Anyone can enjoy the wonder of a sunset as God paints in brilliant colors on the canvas of sky. Take a child on a fishing trip. Catch a lightning bug. Observe a robin weaving a nest. Buy lemonade from the kids on your street. Laugh at yourself. Do lunch with a buddy. Send a card to an elderly person. Fly a kite. Sip hot coffee as the sun comes up. Build a snowman. Care for a pet. Send flowers. Eat your

favorite ice cream cone twice in one day. Plant a tree.
Ride a bike. Attempt something new. Wear something
red. Spice it up a little.

If you will take these things to heart and begin to enjoy life,
you will begin to derive many benefits. You will be
obeying the Bible. You will be happier, live longer and
spread much good cheer. Let us begin to enjoy life. God
has given it to us…it is up to us as to how we spend it. The
good times have not gone away. It may be that the good
times are hidden just beneath your to-do list.

11

SACRIFICE HAS ITS REWARDS, GUARANTEED

Burnout has become a common word in the Christian community. It is because of the hours of effort that seemingly never come to an end. The job is never completed and more work is always needed. In times of such push to achieve, it is easy to lose sight of the rewards that come along with the sacrifice.

Mark 10:28-29 records a conversation between Peter and Jesus. "Then Peter began to mention all that he and the other disciples had left behind. "We've given up everything to follow you," he said. And Jesus replied, "I assure you that everyone who has given up house or brothers or sisters or mother or father or children or property for my sake and the Good News, will receive now in return, a hundred times over, houses, brothers, sisters, mothers, children, and property with persecutions. And in the world to come they will have eternal life."

Evidently Peter had grown weary of the work. He was ready to trade in his Christian work clothes, his ministry and even his walk with the Lord. His words indicate he was ready to return to the old fishing boat, creaking oars, and the smell of fish he had left behind to follow Christ.

I suppose there is not a believer alive who, from time to time, wonders if it might be better back in the 'old boat.' The pressures of service often are draining, leaving little time or energy for self or family. Thoughts of trading one's briefcase for a fishing pole sounds mighty good. Most would jump at a cut in pay for a decrease in pressure. Leave the fish-bowl lifestyle for a jaunt into oblivion? Tempting! These were the temptations of Peter, which provoked him to ask a few questions of Jesus.

The response of Jesus brings a renewed focus for the task at hand. We serve a Master who is more than fair! He has an equitable payment plan built into His company. Remember, we can never out-give God.

Everything you give, each sacrifice you make will be returned to you…in this life! Did you miss it? Jesus said the things you give up for the Gospel in this life would be returned to you a hundredfold! That is the payment plan. That does not include the benefits. Benefits are an important factor in deciding whether to work for an employer or not. The psalmist wrote, "Bless the Lord oh my soul and forget not all His benefits."

Time and space would not permit a list of the innumerable benefits that are derived from serving the Lord. I must mention the retirement. Jesus made it a point to explain that the payment for sacrifice would not all be given in this life. He said eternal life would be attained in the world to come for those who serve Him faithfully.

However, if there were no benefits, nor payment in this life, the assurance of eternal life with Jesus should be enough reimbursement for every hardship we endure.

"What is in it for me?" This would be a good question for those about to begin their Christian journey. The answer is, a lot of sacrifice and much more reward.

There is much toil and tears, but more smiles. There are some weary miles, yet with each one that passes there is a feeling of completing something that will pay off in eternity. There are more blessings than 'stressing.' You will find more friends than foes. Press on my friend.

Do not listen to the howling of Satan who, like a midway carney, promises pleasure and instantaneous fun. His pseudo-pleasures only last for a little season and they disappear.

Conversely, God's promises are true. There are many wonderful things awaiting those who will faithfully serve the Lord, both in this life and the one to come…guaranteed!

12

WHET YOUR APPETITE FOR HEAVENLY FOOD

I am sure every parent has been frustrated at one time or another with a child who had just filled up on suckers and Tootsie Rolls, then turned up their nose at a wonderful, well-balanced dinner. Most parents encourage their children to curb the intake of sweets and junk food at least an hour before dinner. This is a simple way of preparing their appetite or cultivating a slight hunger so the children will develop a taste and appreciation for good food. Spiritually speaking, we all would be well served to nurture a healthy appetite for heavenly food.

The King James Version of Proverbs 27:7 says, "The full soul loatheth an honeycomb; but to the hungry soul every bitter thing is sweet." In other words, the goodness of the food is not necessarily determined by the taste of the food, but rather by the hunger of the one eating.

Once, my father and another man were fishing on a big lake near the Mexico border. Without warning, a storm blew in and by the time they recognized its intensity, they were in trouble. Their little boat was not equipped for the size of waves they were encountering.

Knowing they could not reach shore, they turned for a little island. With their motor running full force, the boat was swamped and they waded ashore. They spent a long, soggy night marooned on the island. For survival, they built a fire and dug out the only food they could salvage from the boat. The food they gathered would not be what you would call a balanced diet. All of their goodies had become fish food except for a bag of soggy Oreo cookies and a jar of pickled okra. A nasty combo meal! For two wet and chilled fishermen, it was like a gourmet dinner! It was all about hunger.

I fear we often treat preaching like a buffet line at Luby's cafeteria. "I will take some of that. No thank you, I do not like that stuff. Yes, give me two of those sweet things." Know what I mean? If the minister speaking does not choose a topic we enjoy, or if he is not highly educated, or if he butchers the King's English, we are prone to turn him off and excuse ourselves from the table.

A cook who has worked hard to prepare a delicious meal is delighted by those who come to the table with a hearty appetite. Every parcel of the Word of the Lord is good. There admittedly are those who can prepare a spiritual meal with more skill than others. If we come with a hunger for God, no soul will go away disappointed. "Blessed are they that hunger…for they shall be filled." The children of Israel only complained of the manna and the quail after it became an everyday, common place occurrence. We must not let the miracle of God's Word become stale to our taste.

Watchman Nee said, "Water always runs downhill and so does the anointing. You can receive from any man's ministry if you are willing to get down low enough."

Allow God to develop in you a healthy appetite for heavenly food. Whether it is coconut cream pie or pickled okra, it will be good if you are hungry enough.

13

BECOMING A SERVANT TO BECOME A SON

Luke Chapter 15 is one of the greatest passages in our Bible. In my estimation, it captures the purity of God's love for mankind. It encompasses the story of the prodigal son.

The young son had visions of grandeur in mind. There were goals to achieve, places to go, people to meet and things to do. After demanding an early inheritance from his father, he set off in search of fun, fame and fortune.

Friends abounded, the wine was sweet and everything was wonderful…until the money ran out. When the cash was gone, the party seemed to evaporate as well. Excitement gave way to survival. Night found the boy with an empty stomach and an aching heart. Perhaps, for the first time in his life he slept under a bridge somewhere. The next morning there was no breakfast, at noon there was no lunch and no dinner that evening. Aimlessly he staggered to a farm. This once pampered boy found himself desiring the slop being fed to filthy swine.

This is where the story changes. The Bible says, "He came to himself." (Verse 17) What caused the change? What made him come to himself? The change came when the boy took his eyes off himself and decided to become a servant (verse 19). He had been filled with self and in due time lost all he had. He remembered home and decided to return to serve others. Maybe you have become entranced by the hypnotic pseudo-excitement of the world and have focused on yourself too long as well. This would be a great day for a spiritual awakening! You see, the story does not end there. Read on…

Back at home, the father was sitting on the front porch watching the sunset and keeping his eyes on the long, gravel road in front of the house. This was an every evening occurrence. But this night was different!

Just before dark, a lonely, stooped figure appeared on the horizon. The father recognized who it was immediately. His reaction was not retaliatory but rather conciliatory. He jumped from the porch, instructing the servants to start supper and told them to bring the best robe and a ring! The yard gate had hardly closed when father and son fell into each other's arms. The stench of the hog pen and the squandered inheritance was not an issue. The issue was the boy was safe at home again. "Please forgive me," sobbed the young son. It was already so…the servant became the son!

14

THE SPRINGBOARD TO SUCCESS MAY BE DISGUISED

Have you ever watched someone on a diving board enjoying the pool on a summer day? Normally they walk out to the end of the board and bounce a couple of times, then are catapulted into the air for a perfect dive. Next time you view this scene, notice the relationship between how low the board is pressed down, to how high the diver springs into the air. The concept will become clear. The lower the board is forced downward, the higher up the person will go.

The same principle is often true in humanity. We commonly assume the trigger for our success is a break in life, an unexpected windfall of money or a helping hand up the ladder. Many times, however, the springboard principle comes into play. The lower you go, the higher you go. Success often comes springing from the valley of defeat.

The prophet Micah made a bold proclamation from an apparent low point in his life. (Chapter 7:8) "Rejoice not against me, O my enemy: when I fall, I shall arise."

This is the perfect illustration. Push me down, and I will bounce back up again. Let us notice he did not say 'if' I fall. Being human we all will come to the realization we have fallen…we are down. Micah said, 'when' I fall. He also did not say, "I hope I can get back up." He made it very clear, "I shall arise!"

Accusations are many times hurled in the face of God's children when they make mistakes. "I thought you were a Christian!" "You are not supposed to make mistakes!" "I told you Christians are phony because I saw brother 'so and so' lose his temper," etc. The accuser is really only admitting his biblical stupidity. Even the Word of God declares in Proverbs 24:16, "For a *just man* falls seven times, and rises up again."

The wise old saying is true, "You can't keep a good man down." The proof of the good is not in whether a man falls down or not, it is whether he gets back up or not.

Now, is this a license for man to sin? Absolutely not! Paul wrote and asked a relevant question, "Shall we continue in sin, that grace may abound?" He then answers the question in the same verse with a resounding, "God forbid!" (Romans 6:1-2) We must be careful not to frustrate God's grace by continuing to live in a fallen state. Everything about God and His church is concerning the business of helping people get back up.

In the sport of boxing there is the 'standing eight count.' In the event a boxer is knocked down or becomes momentarily incapacitated, the referee will come over to the rattled boxer, once he is back on his feet, and count eight seconds. This gives the boxer a moment to gather his wits and regain his focus on the fight.

Every man and woman I have ever known has, or will have, need of a 'standing eight count' from God. It is time to get back up, get your eyes back on your opponent and regain the confidence to start swinging again. If you feel like you have had your face flattened against the mat of life, perhaps this is where you will begin your greatest comeback ever.

Pressing down a Christian is a dangerous thing to do. They always spring up, higher than ever before. 2 Corinthians 4:9 reminds us that we are sometimes "…cast down, but not destroyed."

Friend, your trial is merely the beginning of your greatest triumph. Your test is about to become a testimony. Your ticket to the top may be courtesy of a valley you did not see as a launch pad!

15

A SERMON FROM A BEETLE BUG

I had taken up my usual post on a bench during a rare visit to an outlet mall with my wife. My attention was diverted from the usual flow of people traffic to a solitary figure that caught my eye. This lone figure was not a person, rather it was a critter, a black beetle approximately one and a half inches long.

This critter was slowly, yet steadily, making its way across the mid-way of the mall. My eyes followed as the insect crept across the shiny red, white and gray tiles. Soon the bug made it to the carpeted entrance of a store and stopped as if to contemplate whether or not it should enter. Perhaps it was merely wondering what this strange textured fiber was that he was about to walk upon. As the little fellow hesitated, he was almost stepped on a couple of different times, once by a tennis shoe and once by a boot that had just narrowly missed. The near miss of the boot was enough to encourage him across the line.

The beetle soon disappeared inside the store leaving me alone with my thoughts.

I pondered how out of place the beetle was. Evidently it had gained access to the mall by some mal-adjusted door. However, it had happened and the insect ended up in an unwelcome and unfriendly environment. It must have been strange to hear a constant sound of music, voices and clamor.

You see, beetles are made to live in and around old logs and tree stumps. Their environment consists of a damp forest floor, leaves, dirt and the elements of the season. "Where would the beetle sleep?" I wondered. Perhaps it will cuddle up to a shopping basket or if it was lucky, find a cardboard box in which it could rest.

There is something just as foreign to mankind as the beetle is to the shopping mall. Sin! Sin is an intruder, a trespasser on the original idea God had in mind. In the original setting, God intended man to live in the paradise of Eden.

Paradise consisted of everything man would need physically and also included a regular, daily relationship with God Himself. Adam and Eve's fall, created the mal-adjusted opening that every human being since has automatically walked through.

Do not think it a normal thing that you should be bound by the addictive sins of this world. It is not the intent of God that you should habitually curse and swear. God's normalcy for you does not include continually living under the influence of compulsive behavior. These and all other vices make up an environment for which you were not created.

Let us think about the divine plan for your life. Every man has an inborn need of God. We all have a God-shaped void in our lives that nothing else in the world can fill. Filling that void with God, His Word and His eternal plan for you should be the most natural thing in the world. Instead, many attempt to substitute the satisfaction of their "God-need" with the placebos of this world. Drugs, alcohol, pornography, gambling, etc. are poor substitutes for righteousness, peace and joy.

Why not allow God a chance at making your life the thing it was intended to be?

Be assured, any time a man turns to these earthly substitutes he is as out of place as a beetle bug in a shopping mall.

16

DEFINING THE GOOD LIFE

Personally, I am not a proponent of multi-level marketing or pyramid schemes. Maybe it works for you, but I have met too many people who have been duped by its idea, including myself.

Usually you are invited to a meeting where a big shot is coming to speak. He or she generally has a million-dollar smile, fake hair and lots of diamonds. They have a 'too-good-to-be-true story' of how they were once a poor, working-class person barely squeaking out a living. Since they started selling for such and such a company, they now have more money than they know what to do with. They show pictures of their new home with a pool, their new car, new boat, new beach home, etc. Their offer sounds viable enough. You sign up under them and a portion of your sales goes to their coffers.

You then sign up ten people as direct distributors in your down line. Everything they sell becomes a profit for you. Soon, you will be sitting atop a stack of money as tall as the roof! You will be rich, dress in the finest clothes, have the best of everything and live the good life. Somehow it is never quite that easy.

My question for us today is…just what is the good life? For many, the good life is like the mirage that is always just over the next hill. Is the compilation of things the only requirement to live the good life? Some think true success in life would be to become famous and see their name in lights. Is that when the good life begins?

Is the good life encompassed in the acclaim of winning a championship, securing the Miss Universe title or acquiring an invitation from the 'Who's Who' of politics or the arts?

Let me tell you about a man who started a different type of company where all of His employees live the good life. It is a different type of company. This man doesn't have rags to riches story, rather He tells of being rich and becoming poor for our sakes.

God Almighty left the splendor of heaven, having all the possessions of the world at His disposal, robed Himself in human flesh, was born in a stable and died to save us. His plan for His "employees" is not to attain all, but rather to leave all and follow Him. To be great in His company you must strive to become the least. The pyramid is inverted and His followers do not look to get people under them, but rather to get people over them. He calls it servanthood. To go up, you must humble yourself, deny yourself and prefer your brother.

Sound out of touch? Sounds like something you would shy away from? That may be because you have bought into the same ideology of the parabolic farmer who decided he would tear down his barns and build bigger ones, while never considering his soul. Jesus called the man a fool for neglecting the most important things.

In Mark 8:36-37 Jesus asks two very important questions: "What shall it profit a man if he shall gain the whole world and lose his own soul? Or what shall a man give in exchange for his soul?"

If you had the best of everything, knew everybody, had been everywhere, done it all and yet you did not have a relationship with Jesus Christ, you would be a poor, poor individual.

On the other hand, if you had holes in your jeans, the motor clanked in your old car and the roof leaked on your house, but you knew the saving power of God, you would be rich indeed!

I say the good life is the ability to lay your head on your pillow at night knowing that if Jesus returned for His church, you know you are ready to go with Him. The good life is having true joy in your heart no matter what circumstance of life you find yourself in.

Proverbs 22:4, "By humility and the fear of the Lord are riches, and honor and life."

If that is not the good life, then I don't know what is.

17

DESPISE NOT THE DAY OF SMALL THINGS

One of the biggest mistakes we make as human beings is to overlook that which appears insignificant. We have become programmed to the grandiose and the spectacular to such a degree that, often we fail to enjoy the beauty of that which is plain, simple and small.

If we had been God, all of the trees would have been giant redwoods and all of the flowers would have been sunflowers. More than likely we would have overlooked the fragile dogwood and the tender daisies.

Were we allowed to create, each body of water would have been an ocean with rolling tides and crashing, mighty waves. We may have failed to create a tiny, gurgling stream. There would have been no rolling hills, only mountains reaching to the heights.

If we were allowed to become the judge of all men, only the elite, the rich and famous and those who had achieved great things would be allowed to enter heaven, whilst snubbing the downtrodden and the small in stature. Understand that I am not minimizing the great. Rather, I want us to share an appreciation of the insignificant.

Through history, great inventions have evolved from rather simple and obscure origins. Consider this: A tea kettle singing on the stove was the beginning of the steam engine. A shirt waving on a clothesline was the beginning of a balloon, the forerunner of the Graf Zeppelin. A spider web strung across a garden path suggested the suspension bridge. A lantern swinging in a tower was the beginning of the pendulum. An apple falling from a tree was the cause of discovering the law of gravitation.

In the Bible there is a great deal said about little things. A little leaven ferments the entire lump of dough. Little foxes spoil the vine. On the other hand, a little faith can move mountains and a little salt adds flavor to the whole pot. A little man, Zacchaeus, was singled out by Christ for a personal visit. A little boy's lunch provided a miraculous feeding of 5,000 people.

Jesus always stood in defense of children. Though they are small, they are extremely valuable. Every child you meet holds the potential to change the world. Recently I told my own children that they have the possibility of being anything they want to be. At this juncture of their education, no person in history had more opportunity, more advantage regarding technology, etc., than they do. In other words, I want them to know that they can become as great as they have the discipline to be.

The prophet asks an important question, "Who has despised the day of small things?" Learn to appreciate the little things of life. Ask God for the ability to see potential.

When you view an acorn, through faith, see it as a mighty oak. When you look at your children, believe that you are witnessing a stalwart man or woman of faith. Remember that a single word spoken can build or tear down entire lives. The small is important after all. Have a blessed day!

18

GOD USES BROKEN POTS

A water carrier in India had two large pots, hung on each end of a pole which he carried across his neck. One of the pots had a crack in it, while the other pot was perfect and always delivered a full portion of water at the end of the long walk from the stream to the master's house.

Of course, the perfect pot was proud of its accomplishments, perfect to the end for which it was made. But the poor cracked pot was ashamed of its own imperfection, and miserable that it was able to accomplish only half of what it had been made to do.

After two years, of what it perceived to be a bitter failure, it spoke to the water bearer. "I am ashamed of myself and I want to apologize to you." "Why?" asked the bearer. "What are you ashamed of?"

"I have been able for these past two years, to deliver only half my load because this crack in my side causes water to leak out all the way back to your master's house. Because of my flaw, you have to do all of this work, and you don't get full value from your efforts," the pot said.

The water bearer felt sorry, and said, "As we return to the master's house, I want you to notice the beautiful flowers along the path."

Indeed, as they went up the hill, the cracked pot took notice of the sun warming the beautiful flowers on the side of the path, and this cheered it some. But at the end of the trail, it still felt bad because it had leaked out half its load, and so again it apologized to the bearer for its failure.

The bearer said to the pot, "Did you notice there were flowers only on your side of the path, but not on the other pot's side? I have always known about your flaw, and I planted flower seeds on your side of the path. Every day while we walked back from the stream, you watered them. For two years, I have been able to pick these beautiful flowers to decorate my master's table. Without you being just the way you are, my master would not have this beauty to grace his house."

Each of us has our own unique flaws. We are all cracked pots. Somehow, if we will allow it, the Lord will use our flaws to grace the Kingdom table. Do not be afraid of your flaws. In some way, our weakness will be turned to strength and our ugliness into a thing of beauty!

19

FORGIVENESS IS A GOOD IDEA, UNTIL YOU HAVE TO DO IT

"I can forgive, but I cannot forget' is only another way of saying, "I will not forgive." Forgiveness ought to be like a canceled note: torn in two, and burned up, so that it never can be shown against one." - unknown

This unknown author had keen insight into a very important subject, forgiveness. Forgiveness is a two-way street. You give and you receive it. According to the Lord Jesus, each direction on this street is relative. Let me explain.

First, when you forgive someone who has treated you in an ill or unfair manner, you release yourself from bad feelings. Often, the person needing forgiveness may never ask for it and may not, in your opinion, deserve it. Willful forgiveness is a key that sets you free.

Secondly, Jesus taught us that we must forgive in order to be forgiven.

In Matthew 6:12, Christ demonstrated how we should pray by saying, "Forgive us our debts, as we forgive our debtors." Further, in verses 14-15, He said, "For if you will forgive men their trespasses, your heavenly Father will also forgive you; but if you do not forgive men their trespasses, neither will your Father forgive your trespasses."

Do you see the connection? Recall the example left for us by Jesus. His very life and death were lessons in forgiveness. When a group of vindictive, bloodthirsty men cast an adulterer at His feet, He simply said, "Let he that is without sin, first cast a stone." To the woman caught in the sinful act He said, "Neither do I condemn you, go and sin no more."

Oh, that you and I could ascertain the spirit of a forgiver. I know from experience it is much easier at first to strike back, to want to get even and to settle the score. In Christianity, taking the low road is the righteous road. Someone once stated, "Inflicting an injury puts you below your enemy; revenging one, makes you even with him; forgiving him, sets you above him."

Notice in Jesus' death, He looked into the eyes of the very men who were murdering Him and prayed, "Father forgive them, for they know not what they do."

Many times, I have discovered that true forgiveness does not occur until I am willing to pray for and even bless the person who was in the wrong. By calling their name to God and saying, "I forgive," you will find a powerful release of bad feelings.

I can promise you this is one area of life you will absolutely get to practice. When your turn rolls around, I hope you will remember the freedom that is felt when you are forgiven and have the goodness about you to pass it on to someone else. When it comes to forgiveness, it is always much easier to receive. That is why I say, forgiveness is a good idea, until you have to do it. So, when it is time to bury the hatchet, do not bury it in your neighbor's back! May you and yours enjoy the blessings of God this week.

20

TRUE FRIENDS ARE RARE AND VALUABLE

The historian Henry Brooks Adams once wrote, "One friend in a lifetime is much; two are many; three are hardly possible." The older I get, the more I have come to understand the incredible rarity and value of having a true friend.

I suppose there are varying degrees of friendships. Acquaintances are the people you know by name and face. There are neighbors who strike up friendships, watching out for one another's interests. People with whom you share a similar hobby or vocation are often put on the friend list. Co-workers and those who enjoy a shared activity without intimacy are considered friends. Even relatives fall into this category.

The next category includes friendships that go beyond the casual. These are true friends that you are able to be your real self in their presence, whether you are up or down, rich or broke. Pogrebin writes, "Friendship is a heart-flooding feeling that can happen to any two people who are caught up in the act of being themselves, together, and who like what they see."

We know friendships are important because of their enriching value and genuine assistance brought to our lives.

Further, the Bible has much to say about friendships. Let us take a closer look at the wisdom of the Word of God regarding this important subject.

Proverbs 18:24, "A man that has friends must show himself friendly." The blame for being without a close friend does not lie in the lap of others. We can only look at ourselves. Winning a friendship requires that you reach outside your zone of comfort and demonstrate a willingness to make a friend.

Proverbs 6:3 gives instruction for maintaining a friendship. "Go, humble thyself and make sure thy friend." To me, the way to keep a friendship intact is to never wait for your friend to make the next gesture. You should be willing to always initiate good will.

Proverbs 17:17 is perhaps the greatest definition of a friend. "A friend loves at all times and a brother is born for adversity." A true friend is one that will not duck and run, even if everyone else is against you. Jonathan's willingness to protect David from the wrath of Saul is a perfect example.

I have found that adversity usually weeds out the fair-weather friends or those who befriend you only for what they can get from you. A man with money and a good time will have a bounty of 'good friends.' On the other hand, when the chips are down and the struggles of life are looming, you find out who is 'true blue.'

I pray that you are blessed with many real friends in this life. However, if you do not have friends, and you feel totally alone, I want to point you to One who would love to become your best friend. His Name is Jesus. John 15:13-14 states, "Greater love hath no man than this, that a man would lay down his life for his friends. You are my friends, if you do whatever I commanded you."

Jesus Christ has already demonstrated His willingness to be your friend. He laid down His life on the cross. You can now demonstrate your desire to be His friend by obeying His desire for your life.

The Seri Indians of Northern Mexico have no word in their vocabulary for the word "friend." Friendly relationships do not appear to exist among them. Can you imagine how cold the world would be without a friend?

The words 'friend' and 'free' come from the same root word, suggesting that one aspect of friendship is the freedom to be ourselves. "A friend," said Ralph Waldo Emerson, "is a person with whom I may be sincere." My prayer is that you would first find Jesus Christ to be your friend and then to find in your life, at least one person who you could trust as a true friend.

21

HONKING YOUR HORN CHANGES ONLY DECIBEL LEVELS, NOT CIRCUMSTANCES

Last week I happened on a scene that is so representative of the culture in which we live. An elderly man had pulled up to a stop sign, where the street he was traveling intersected a highway. He needed to turn left, thus mandating that he would have to maneuver both lanes of traffic. The highway was busy that afternoon in both directions.

Since there was no traffic light to help the man out, he was forced to watch for an opening, which obviously was much slower materializing than he expected. Evidently the man had sat there until his patience had run out – faster than the speeding traffic in front of him. I approached the intersection from the highway, signaled and began to slow for the turn. Suddenly, the old man could take it no more. He just began blaring his horn!

With no one at fault and no one attacking him, he simply could not hold his peace any longer at the brutal wall of traffic impeding his life. The sudden extinction of his patience was proven by his all-too-frequent use of that handy little feature in the center of his steering wheel. So, he just honked! He honked at cars, trucks, the clouds…the world!

Now, I must admit that I am a little ornery at times. I was somewhat humored at the fact this this guy was now blowing his horn at me…and I had done absolutely nothing wrong! As I turned in front of him, I stopped my truck in such a fashion that he could not help but look at me eye to eye. Rolling down my window, I asked if there was a problem. He quit looking at me, attained a rather sheepish, 'deer in the headlights' appearance and then looked the other way.

Although the man must have assumed I was an arrogant jerk wanting to start some trouble, I really understood the man better than he could have ever known. Why? It's because I blow my horn too! Oh yes, and you do too! Maybe not literally, but in some ways we all blow our horns. We honk our frustrations in a variety of ways.

The honks come when we run out of options, are trapped at the intersection of life and nobody will seem to give us a break to let us in the flow of humanity. When life cannot be normal; when the unexpected bills come with no money to cover them; when you get sick of wearing a plastic happy face while your heart is breaking; when you absorb yourself in work to get ahead and things only turn out worse; when people look to you as someone in control…the ultimate success…and inside you feel miserable; when your children are shunned for no wrongdoing of their own; when you get cancer and never smoked a cigarette…and the list goes on and on. In these moments, life careens out of control and, since you cannot fix the problem, you turn to your only alternative…lay on

that horn, baby! Let the whole wide world know that you
have been duped, drilled, drained and dried!

Horn honking is merely an attempt to tell those around you
of the pain inside. Classic horn blowing comes in various
forms, such as physical violence, drug or alcohol abuse, fits
of rage and wrath, becoming critical of others, suicide
attempts or severe deviations from normal behavior. I
would venture to say the majority of those who occupy our
prison systems are those who, somewhere in their lives,
attempted to first cry out for help by sending one or more
of the above signals.

Observe the following 'horn blowing facts.' 1. Honking
your horn does not change the traffic on the highway!
Honking creates an annoying noise, but does nothing
toward solution. 2. Honking creates negative feelings in
those around you! Expressing pain in a negative way only
serves to hurt those around you. 3. Honking will bring
unwanted attention from those around you, which will add
to your problems. Once I was selected for jury duty in a
case where road rage at a stop sign ended up in a shooting.

So, what do you do when you are trapped at the stop sign of
life? The only answer I can give is one that none of us
enjoy hearing. It is to wait! God usually answers in one of
three ways – yes, no and wait! More often than not, it is
the third answer because it is good for us and it allows God
the time to work His perfect will that we, or others, have
messed up in haste. Psalm 27:14, "Wait patiently on the
Lord: Be brave and courageous. Yes, wait patiently for the

Lord." Psalm 40:1 tells the result of such waiting, "I waited patiently for the Lord to help me, and He turned to me and heard my cry."

Friend, all you can do is to wait. If you will be patient, sooner or later, the highway will clear, it will be your turn and you can get back on your way. Until then, lay off the horn – it is much safer that way!

22

ONE BABY CHANGED THE WORLD

In 1970 the most fierce and modern warship of the U.S. Naval Fleet sailed across the North Atlantic Ocean. The USS John F. Kennedy was an aircraft carrier, equal in length to three and one half football fields and carrying a staggering 6,000 troops aboard. Operational demands were comparable to a small city.

Life at sea can become rather boring. The routine of living aboard ship can fall into the category of monotonous after weeks at sea. Repetitious jobs and meals had caused the men to assume a rather melancholy attitude. That is when the package arrived! A young signal corpsman, also known as a skivvy waver, received a care package from home with a bag of Jiffy Pop popcorn included. So, down to his berth he went, where he had a hot plate in his personal possessions. On the hot plate, he placed his Jiffy Pop and soon had a steaming bag of fresh popcorn from home.

But that is not all he had. He also had a literal mob on his hands! Unbeknownst to him, the smell of his single bag of popcorn had drifted into the common ventilator system and had been carried throughout the ship. Sailors from all over the ship started looking for the source of a wonderful smell that reminded them of the comforts of home.

Like wildfire across an open prairie, the desire for popcorn began to rage. There was none to be found on the ship anywhere! More than the fact that the men liked popcorn, was the fact that they could not get any.

The lack of supply was creating an overabundance of demand. The smell of fresh popcorn not only contaminated the ventilation system, it also contaminated the minds of everyone on board. The men could not think straight! Production went down! Morale dropped! Everyone from the brass and the pilots, to the men swabbing the deck, had roasted kernels on their minds. For the want of popcorn, the most awesome war vessel in the world was brought to a virtual halt.

So, the captain sent out a call for popcorn. Helicopters brought pallets of it! Other ships pulled alongside and tossed over 50-pound bags of popcorn. One entire galley was shut down for 48 hours for the sole purpose of popping popcorn. That heavenly fragrance of 'home sweet home' filled every cubicle of the ship. Sailors poured out of their bunks with pillow cases that would soon serve as popcorn sacks. It was the mother of all popcorn parties! Every person had his fill. Morale went up, and the carrier sailed away with a very happy crew.

Just over 2,000 years ago there was a world adrift in the ocean of time. Mankind had become so preoccupied with himself and his sin that he had forgotten about home. That is until the prophets began to write about "a child that would be born who would save his people from their sins." At the hint of such an idea, the world longed for such. Just think of a Messiah, a Redeemer who would rectify the fallen, depraved status of sinful man. It 'smelled' good! A craving was created in the spiritual appetite. However, these were mere prophecies until the miracle of Bethlehem. Here the plan unfolds. "In the fullness of time, God sent forth His Son." The invisible God of eternity became visible and the recognition of our need became evident. Like the solitary sailor with a small bag of popcorn, it began in obscurity, in a lowly manger. Soon the desire for a Savior began spreading. At first, it drew common shepherds. Next, wise men were loading expensive gifts and leaving their abodes to find this Blessed One. In short time, everything was affected. Angels were bursting forth with song in the heavenlies! A new and awesome star was shining with brilliance.

Through the Word of God taught by Sunday School teachers, missionaries, and ministers of every sort, the world is getting a whiff of something none of us can really live without. It is salvation! The good news is, there is plenty and the party is just starting! No one has to leave this life without partaking. An invitation from an old rugged cross is still in effect for "…whosoever will." It is the free gift of God, eternal life, the reason for Christmas. Perhaps the angel said it best, "Born to you this day in the City of David is a Savior, Christ the Lord."

23

BARABBAS' STORY IS EASILY MISSED, BUT IS STILL RELEVANT

The story of Barabbas is easily overlooked in scripture. It should not be, because we all have so much in common with it. Recall this old story with me...a few details added to fill out the story.

His very name, Bar-abbas, gives a little insight into this man. Let us break this down a little. 'Bar,' means "the son of," and 'Abbas,' which was no doubt his father's name; hence, the son of Abbas. Abbas was a common name among the wealthy and religious folk of the day. It is possible that Barabbas was reared in a righteous home. As is often the case, he lost his way, had his way, and ultimately made his way to a prison cell with the pronouncement of a death sentence.

Try to imagine Barabbas' final night before the day Jesus was crucified. It is easy to imagine him sitting on the cold, damp floor of his cell saying to himself, "Tonight is my last night on earth. Before this time tomorrow, they will nail my body, by my hands and feet, to a public torture post or cross."

Perhaps a shiver ran down his spine as he could almost hear the gruesome snapping of his leg bones when Roman soldiers would crush them with an iron bar. "Worse," he thought, "is the thought of going to my eternal judgment with all these crimes on my record."

It is possible that his family was permitted to see him on that final night. His father's bitter tears at raising such a failure must have been almost unbearable. The familiar smell of his mother's perfume and the fearful look in his own children's eyes would linger long after the sobbing parade had exited the jail.

Sleep would not come easy this night. He could hear someone working late in the prison yard. They were hammering on something. He assumed it must be his cross. Just about the time he dozed off, footsteps of the guards would quickly push back the fog of his weary mind, causing his heart to pump wildly. Were they coming for him?

As morning light peeked through the window and penciled shadowy lines across the cell floor, he says to himself, "This is the day…my very last…soon they will open that door and take me to my death." Suddenly, he hears noise from the hall. It is different this time. A distinct rustle of sandals, jingle of keys, tapping of spears on rock floors and muffled voices, fill the atmosphere. This is truly it, no mistake about it! His mouth is dry. A bead of cold sweat trickles down his forehead into his thick, black eyebrows. A key turns in a rusty lock. The door swings open to view a small band of strong, young soldiers. Goodbye to life and hope! Death, only death, ahead now, and after death what will there be?

The ranking officer speaks, "Barabbas, today is your lucky day. You are a free man!" These words make very little impression on him.

"I am in no mood for jokes!" he scoffs. He can take no more and screams at the armed group, "Do not make fun of me! Get this over with, take me to the hill and kill me, but do not rip my soul to pieces!"

Again, the officer growls, "YOU ARE FREE! The door is open, go out, go home!" The dawning truth is so wonderful he can hardly believe it. Outside he hears the crowd still chanting, "Give us Barabbas!" and he begins to understand his escape from the dreadful clutches of Roman law. The soldiers tell him of Pilate's custom to set one man free on this day. The Jews have chosen him instead of Jesus of Nazareth.

Barabbas begins to cry like a child with a broken heart. He knows who Jesus is. He saw many of His miracles. While Jesus was feeding 5,000 people, he was rifling through the boats anchored along the shore stealing nets and knives! It is more than he can absorb to realize a just man will die in the place of a thief and murderer.

We should all feel as Barabbas likely felt. First, that we are sinners and deserve death. Secondly, we should feel humbled that our lives were saved at such an awful cost. If Christ had not taken our place, we also would be serving an eternal death sentence.

24

RAISING TEENS REQUIRES GENTLE PRESSURES

Careful is the key word when raising teenagers. This is especially true when giving advice about them. (I have a couple of them at home at this writing!) Since the jury is still out, I will offer this advice for myself and anyone else who may be able to use it.

If you have ever worn braces on your teeth, you understand the philosophy of pressure. It is constant, gentle pressures, at just the right points and angles, that one day yield a beautiful smile. When the braces are tightened there is pain for a day or two, then it goes away with the adjustment of the teeth. A perfect set of ivories does not occur overnight, but over time. So it is with raising teenagers. Do not despair if everything you have tried to teach them seems lost in a maze of mixed emotions and behaviors. Keep the pressure on…gently.

The teenage years can be especially difficult because they require a different tact of training and discipline than used in the earlier, formative years. When your child was small, you gave him distinct boundaries and enforced them with a sharp 'no-no' and/or a curt slap to the wrist or the backside of the lap. As they change, so must the methods.

Scripture says in Proverbs 22:6, "Train up a child in the way he should go: and when he is old, he will not depart from it." If you have a child who grows up and never strays from the righteous path, you are a blessed individual. The reality is however, most children reach a point in their mid to late teens where they try to establish their own identity.

They are in a whirlpool of thought, ideas, hormones, etc, - a poor environment for healthy thinking or good choices. The very last thing they need at that critical point in their lives is a parent to add more, unrealistic, harsh expectations. They feel an urge to try their wings, and guess what…they will not do it like you think they should. Count on it. You probably will not like their music or their style. Your help, at that point, must be in the form of a steady, well-balanced reference point.

This delicate balance is struck by knowing when to give and when to take. I believe good parents see themselves as coaches rather than bosses. Using the concept of rewards is more powerful than the concept of prevention. By that I mean, reinforce the good, positive behavior in a big way! When they cross the line toward negative friends or behaviors, a persistent loving pressure away from the evil is the best means of curbing it. Talk to your teen as an adult. Respect them and they often will thank you by living up to your respect.

Many people err in raising children by failing to give them the three T's as an adolescent child: Training, Time and

Trust. It is absolutely ludicrous to fail in the early years, allowing their 'teeth of character and conduct' to grow crookedly, and then expect you can straighten everything out overnight! The idea of Proverbs 22:6 is to train the child or keep the pressure on over a protracted period of time. Remember, "As the tree is bent, so grows the tree!"

Many years ago, British pastor John Patton gave his Sunday night congregation this advice about becoming pals with their children: "Thirty years divide a father and son. Each looks out on the world with his own eyes, and sees things from his own view point. Is it any wonder that misunderstandings sometimes arise? Be the pal of your boy."

Be employing these principles, we can see our children develop into wonderful, productive citizens who honor God by loving their own children one day.

25

THE WORDS OF AN OLD HYMN ISSUE A CHALLENGE

Every Christian has a responsibility to assist others in their attempt to find the Lord. The CEO for Motel 6, Tom Bodette, always concluded his advertisement with the catch phrase, "We'll leave the light on for you." Similarly, the Christian is challenged by Christ to be the light of the world. Those lost in the darkness of addiction, occultism and sins of various form, need a light to help find their way home.

In the mid 1800's, Philip Bliss penned the words to a beautiful, old hymn whose words and tune have blessed the hearts of believers for many years. The song entitled, "Let the Lower Lights be Burning," was written after Bliss heard a stirring message by the great evangelist, D. L. Moody. During the sermon, an illustration was given that went something like this:

On a dark, stormy night when the waves rolled like mountains and not a star could be seen, a large passenger boat cautiously edged toward the Cleveland harbor.

The pilot knew that, in the inky darkness, he could only find the harbor channel by keeping two lower shore lights in line with the main beacon. "Are you sure this is

Cleveland?" asked the captain, seeing only one light from the lighthouse.

"Quite sure, sir," replied the pilot.
"Where are the lower lights?" he asked.

"Gone out, sir," was the reply.

"Can you make the harbor?"

"We must or perish, sir!"

With a strong hand and a brave heart, the old pilot turned the wheel. But alas! In the darkness he missed the channel, the boat crashed on the rocks. And many lives were lost.

D. L. Moody's closing words were: "Brethren, the Master will take care of the great lighthouse; let us keep the lower lights burning."

Such wisdom is appropriate today. God will keep His light burning around the world. Because we cannot single-handedly change the entire world does not excuse us from influencing any part we can, whether big or small. By doing what we can, wherever we can, we will indeed help to change the world!

Here are the words to Philip Bliss's great hymn:

Brightly beams our Father's mercy,
From His lighthouse evermore,
But to us, He gives the keeping,
Of the lights along the shore.

Dark the night of sin has settled,
Loud the angry billows roar,
Eager eyes are watching, longing,
For the lights along the shore.

Trim your feeble lamp, my brother,
Some poor sailor tempest-tossed,
Trying now to make the harbor,
In the darkness may be lost.

Let the lower lights be burning!
Send a gleam across the wave!
Some poor fainting, struggling seaman,
You may rescue, you may save.

Send out illuminating beams of the gospel light everywhere you go! Have a wonderful week!

26

HAVE YOU MET MR. SPIEGEL?

"Mirror, mirror on the wall, who's the fairest of them all?" This famous line from the fairy tale *Snow White and the Seven Dwarfs* was the cause of much hatred from the old witch. The mirror told the truth and she would not accept the fact that she had lost her place as the most beautiful woman in the land. We all must face the mirror and the truth at some point in our lives.

Missionary Jim Green left his job and homeland to share the gospel with Germany. It was no small sacrifice as he took with him four children and a wife.

Before leaving the United States, he felt the Lord speak to him that he would meet a "Mr. Spiegel" and he would be part of the reason he went to Germany. During his tenure overseas, he constantly looked for and hoped to meet Mr. Spiegel. The work and the language were often very difficult and the results were not as swift in coming as he had hoped they would be. In his heart he knew if he could ever meet this mystery man, things would change and a great revival would result. However, he kept on praying, preaching and reaching out to the German people, but never once did he come in contact with the Mr. Spiegel he so longed to meet.

One morning, the missionary got up and went into the bathroom to shave. While standing in front of the mirror, he began rehearsing some of the language he was learning. It occurred to him that the German word for mirror is "spiegel." In a moment, the picture became clear. The Mr. Spiegel he was to meet was the man in the mirror. God sent him half way around the globe to help him find himself! After that, a healthy church was established that continues to thrive to this day.

What about you? Are you hiding from the person in the mirror? Have you really come to terms with who you are? With your purpose for existing? With your failures? With your possibilities? I dare say, most people really have never met the real Mr. Spiegel.

James 1:23-24 states, "Anyone who listens to the word but does not do what it says is like a man who looks at his face in a mirror and, after looking at himself, goes away and immediately forgets what he looks like."

The Word of God forces us to ask the hard questions. "Does the man in your heart match the man in the mirror?" More often than not, the two do not match. There are many reasons why. One is, our society expects us to keep our happy face on at all times. We wear masks and tell each other how fantastic we are doing when asked, yet when we are alone, we cope by popping our pills, drinking our drinks or engaging in activities until we are numbed to the pain of reality. Other reasons include the situations of life which are beyond our control. These negative events often create a truth gap between the person on the outside and the one within.

Perhaps the greatest personal revival any of us will ever enjoy will only happen after having a good, honest meeting with the man in the mirror. Our young people today might say it this way, "Get real!"

John 8:32 lends an important promise, "You will know the truth, and the truth will set you free." Schedule an appointment with Mr. Spiegel today. May the Lord bless you and make His face to shine upon you this week!

27

NO TRIP TOO ROUGH TO OUTWEIGH THE REWARD OF REACHING JESUS

A paper in Memphis, Tennessee, reported the story of an amazing dog several years ago. The dog was a fox terrier whose name was Tiny. Tiny was owned by a Mr. M. E. Rainey, a Knoxville grocer. One day he gave the dog to a friend who was moving to New Orleans, Louisiana. Shortly after the friend's arrival in Louisiana, Mr. Rainey got a letter saying that Tiny had disappeared. One night, as Mr. Rainey was preparing to lock up his store, he heard a scratching at the door. He opened it and there, to his amazement, he saw Tiny who was now thin and bedraggled, wearily wagging his tail. It had taken Tiny eleven weeks and three days to make the trip, which is seven hundred, seventy-one miles by highway! Such an incredible journey could only be explained by a love for his master. Nothing would stop this little animal from returning to the one he loved – not weather, not distance, not anything.

Oh, that we all had such a love in our hearts for God! There is no doubt about the things in life we love. They are revealed by the amount of time, money and energy we spend to do them, get them and enjoy them. Some love their cars, their lawns, their hobbies or their positions more than they love the most important thing in life…God. He commands us to love Him with everything we possess.

If we learn to love Jesus in such a manner, nothing in this world will prevent us from getting to Him. For the love of God, no distance is too great, no difficulty too extreme and no night too dark to prevent our finding the way to His loving arms. In learning to love the Lord, we find that He helps us through our storms.

Like Tiny, we look beyond the pain of the moment knowing that the soothing arms of our Friend will one day be worthy everything we go through. A loving relationship with the Lord is the very thing that qualifies one as being a Christian.

The commandments of God in the New Testament are to love the Lord thy God with all thy heart, soul, mind and strength and to love our neighbor as ourselves. Christians of the first and second centuries endured much hardship. History's pages are bloodied with the lives of countless men and women who gave their lives for the sake of the Gospel.

I urge you to renew your love for our Lord. It will become a burning passion that will drive you beyond your fears, your tears and your disappointments. One look at the face of the Master will make all the miles worth it!

28

THE BIBLE TELLS US THE REST OF THE STORY

Paul Harvey had a radio program of wonderful stories filled with almost unimaginable twists and turns. He called the program, "The Rest of the Story." Through study of the Bible, we witness the individual lives of its characters and learn to make right decisions from their successes and failures. In this sense, they were truly "...written for our examples." (I Corinthians 10:11) Thus, we are privy to the 'rest of the story.'

Two of the gospels record the account of one known only as the "rich, young ruler" who came to Jesus for salvation. Notice, he was first rich, meaning he had many possessions. Not only was he rich, he was young. These two qualities are usually not used in the same sentence unless someone is very lucky or has uncanny abilities and wisdom beyond their years. Obviously, the first reason for his early success can be eliminated because this particular young man is also noted as being a 'ruler.' Young rulers are in office not because of blind luck, but because of their wisdom. Evidently, this man was a tremendous oddity. He was rich, young, smart and very principled, making him rarer still. By his own admission, he confessed to Christ of having kept the commandments of God from his childhood.

In Jesus' discourse with the young man, He told him he still lacked "one thing" in order to merit eternal life. "Go and sell all you have and give the money to the poor, and you will have treasure in heaven. Then come follow Me." You would think a man with rigorous religious training would be more than ready to follow the commands of the Master. Instead, the young man began to imagine a mental inventory of all his possessions. "Let us see, that means I will have to give up my new boat, my custom home, my 401K retirement, my stocks, my herd of registered oxen and my late model chariot." The price, at the moment, seemed too high to pay. So, scripture said, "At this, the man's face fell, and he went sadly away because he had many possessions."

For many, the things of mortal life mean more than the things of God. An apt question is directed at all mankind from Holy scripture, "What shall it profit a man if he gains the whole world and loses his soul?" (Matthew 16:26) Clearly, nothing in this material world is worth the loss of eternal life.

Fast forward now in scripture to the 14th chapter of Mark's gospel. Onto the Bible stage enters, or perhaps 're-enters,' a character for merely two verses in scripture. Nothing in God's Word is accidental. These two seemingly insignificant verses may hold a wealth of information. (See verses 51-52) The scene unfolds in the Garden of Gethsemane, the location of Jesus' arrest. Jesus had taken His disciples there to pray before His crucifixion. In this context we find the following: "There was a young man following along behind, clothed only in a linen nightshirt. When the mob tried to grab him, they tore off his clothes, but he escaped and ran away naked."

Because of the specificity of the text, I believe it is possible we are reading about the same "young man" who previously could not follow Jesus because of the cost, which seemed too high to pay. Now, from the shadows, he has followed all the way to the place of Christ's arrest in the garden. Is it possible the young man hid in the underbrush and witnessed the excruciating prayer of the God-man as He cried out, "Let this cup pass from Me?" Did the 'boy wonder' say "Amen" to the eternal words of Jesus, "Nevertheless, not My will but Thy will be done?" Did the rich, young ruler watch with regret as sweat, like droplets of blood, formed on the brow of the Lord?

Here too is an interesting point. At this mention of the young man, all he has in his possession was a single linen garment. Did he finally come to the place where he decided to give it all away? Did he acquiesce to the demands of salvation? If so, here is the 'rest of the story' that is unspoken.

Like Abraham of old, when asked to give his son on the altar of sacrifice, the angel stopped him when he saw that the old prophet was willing to surrender his greatest possession. I believe it is likely that the same God would have done the same thing in the New Testament. Had the rich, young ruler been willing to give up his earthly possessions, the Lord may have allowed him to keep them.

However, he did not stay around for the rest of Jesus' sermon in Mark 10:29-30, "I assure you that everyone who has given up house or brothers or sisters or mother or father or children or property, for My sake and for the Good News, will receive now in return, a hundred times over, houses, brothers, sisters, mothers, children and property...and in the world to come they will have eternal life." The rich young ruler could have been a modern-day Job who lost it all, but wound up better and richer in the end.

When God asks something of you, be prepared to surrender it. What you give up now, you will likely get back later on, and possibly more in the end. An old saying reminds, "He is no fool who gives what he cannot keep to gain what he cannot lose." And now you know...the rest of the story. Have a blessed day!

29

WALK IN 'MOCCASIN MILES' BEFORE JUDGING

A familiar old quote says, "Don't judge a man until you have walked a mile in his moccasins." Moccasins were traditionally crude, leather shoes worn by American Indians. Their thin soles allowed the wearer to feel every pebble or stick beneath his foot, proving especially beneficial while silently stalking animals during hunts for food. The moral of the proverb is to remind us not to judge a man until we put ourselves in his place and understand the position from which he or she is coming. The reason for wearing their moccasins, instead of boots, is so that we may be able to feel, through their 'souls,' everything they have felt.

First impressions and snap judgments are almost always incorrect. There are at least two things you will learn by slipping on someone else's moccasins. One, you will discover that a mile is a long way to go on the hoof! Even small weights get heavy over a protracted period of time. Two, more often than not, the moccasins will be too tight, too loose, too run over at the heel, too 'something' for our feet. The point being, everyone has their own unique set of circumstances by which life has forced them to live, the largest portion we, from the outside looking in, will never know about.

The same is true around the church. I have heard or seen critics send signals that said, "I wish someone would take control of these wild kids." "So-and-so thinks she is something because she has the lead part in the song." "There is no need for John Doe to be so boisterous in his worship!" "Why in the world does that person cry all the time in church? They must be weak-minded!" Before you let the gavel fall, take a moment to consider the reasons and motives from which the criticized base their actions. In other words, slip into their moccasins and hike their trail for a mile or so.

Have you considered that many of the children who may come to your church, on the bus or otherwise, are from broken homes? Most have felt the pain and insecurity of seeing their parents fight and ultimately their homes ripped apart. Some have been victims of all types of abuse. When they get to church, it may be the only safe haven they have where they can express themselves without fear…thus their behavior. Perhaps you are unaware of how much prayer it has taken for the lady who sings, to overcome the pains of her past. You may not have noticed the tears poured out in private, the only thing that gives her strength to stand in front of a congregation of people. For you, it may be easy and natural. For her, there may be a huge cost involved! It could be that a mile in the moccasins of the man who worships God with all his might, would have been a continual trail to and from the liquor store or the drug lord a few years ago. Rather than criticize, understand his trail of tears has led him to give all to Jesus. Before silently judging the person who often weeps, consider that his or her children may not be sitting on the church pew as yours are. Their heart may be broken for the sake of their own flesh and blood, who remain outside the ark of safety.

Remember David and his summons of Uriah the Hittite from the battlefield? While David stayed home from the battle, Uriah refused to sleep in the comforts of his own home upon his return. Although he could have been in the warmth of his own bed, he chose to sleep outside on the ground. His brethren were still on the war-front sleeping in dirty foxholes, risking their lives. Uriah could not be self-serving when others were in a difficult spot. He, in essence, kept their moccasins on! This empathetic gesture would serve us all well.

Instead of being the ultimate critic, defer judgment and consider that there are likely reasons for the behaviors of everyone. This certainly is not to infer the justification of sin, but be assured behind every face is a little more pain, a little more sorrow, a little more disappointment than any of us ever could know. One day you will appreciate someone who will slip into your 'skins' and walk a few paces attempting to understand your actions. 'Moccasin Miles' teach us tolerance, patience and sympathy.

30

GOD WILL BRING GOOD FROM THE STORM

Two magazines lay side by side on the counter, both displaying pictures detailing the landscape of ocean-front scenery. If I were to ask you to describe what articles may be found in the pictures, you would most likely describe palm trees, a sunset, or sandy beaches – complete with shells, starfish and a sailboat in the background. The truth is, you would be describing only one of the two tabloids. One of the books advertises cruises. Its cover is donned by a lovely, sun-tanned couple who appear to have never had a worry in their lives. The other magazine is not so pleasant, as you may have guessed. As a news periodical, its cover discloses the horrors and devastation of Hurricane Katrina as it attempted to rip the soul out of New Orleans!

By now, we have all witnessed the graphic pictures, the daring rescues and almost unbelievable reality, from the heartbreaking to the heroic. We are left to grapple with a host of questions that automatically spring into mind.

Why did such a storm occur? Was it a judgmental act of God upon a wicked city or a freak of nature, spawned by an aging environment? Why did not more people evacuate ahead of the storm? Why did emergency assistance respond so slowly? Can New Orleans rebuild, or should they? How will families who have lost everything put their lives together again? These are questions without appropriate answers. However, I can reassure you that, from the rubble of the rumble, God will see that much good will be the result.

God's Word is a book of precedent from which we can view many storms and witness their ultimate outcomes. The various stories contain winds ranging from gentle to vicious. Mankind, from every age, has had to weather the effects of these storms. Great storms have reduced the brilliance of the human mind as well as the skills of man and machine to near nothing. Great buildings have been shaken to powder and huge ships have been tossed as toys on the billowing waves. Afterward, we are left to wonder, to rebuild and to admit our weaknesses.

The Bible renders the familiar account of Jonah and the storm sent to arrest the attention of the drifting prophet. After the storm, there were many positive results. A man returned to his calling and a city was saved! Another time, Jesus sailed along with the disciples and was fast asleep in the boat as waves grew so large their vessel was totally engulfed in water. It did not make sense at the time! Why would Jesus' own have to endure gale-force winds, drenching rain and come face to face with death? Hidden to the eyes of the mortal is the fact that God had His reasons. When the storm was subdued by the Wave-

Walker, a realization of the supernatural always dawned afresh in the hearts of Christ's followers.

Paul suffered many storms and shipwrecks. He washed ashore clinging to the remains of a boat. Through the storm, God brought validity to the message Paul was preaching to an unbelieving audience.

"How does that apply to us?" you might ask. The answer, quite simply, is there will be much good brought from the tragic storm. It may take years to see the full benefit, yet, despite the loss, the net end will be positive. Since the storm, there have been many positive things happen. People all over America are pulling together, as they did during 9/11, to help and lend assistance. I would put our wonderful community right alongside the very best of them! Our guests from New Orleans have felt care from our city. I overheard one guest saying, "God brought me here to see how life ought to be lived."

31

COOKIE-CUTTER CHRISTIANS

During Fall we enjoy the changing of the leaves. It seems that God expresses Himself by dipping His divine paintbrush into hues of yellow and orange, as He paints the trees with artistic precision. Each tree is completely different. Some are colored only on the tops, some only on the tips of the leaves, while others seem to acquire a complete makeover! One thing you will notice is that each one is completely unique from all the others…and so it is with the unique expressions of man.

Each person was made in the image of God. We know that Jesus Christ "…is the image of the invisible God" (Colossians 1:15), meaning, the invisible Spirit of the Father was manifest in the flesh of the Son. When creating the first man, God may have looked through time to His own earthly image and used that as the pattern or prototype for forming Adam. Recall with me that stars and plants were "spoken" into being, but Adam was "formed" from the dust of the ground much like a child would configure things with playdoh. One need only look around to see that God had a creative heyday when He created us! May I tell you God continues to enjoy the creative uniqueness with which He made us and expects us to continually celebrate it?

During the holidays, my sweet grandmother made wonderful cookies for all her grandkids. I always enjoyed watching her cut the cookies from the dough with a cookie-cutter. The cookie-cutter ensures all the cookies are exactly the same size and look exactly alike. As much as I love the cookies, I am glad God did not use a cookie-cutter when making you and me. The DNA of our person, dictates that the color of our hair, color of our eyes, our height, our laugh, our voice, etc. is completely unique from anyone else in the world! Imagine how utterly bland the world would be if everyone were the same. Be assured, God does not want a cookie-cutter church, with cookie-cutter people, wearing cookie-cutter uniforms, who sing cookie-cutter songs, preaching cookie-cutter sermons and…you get the point!

Within the bounds of righteousness, mankind should celebrate his individuality. Man is made to complement the creative bouquet of unique trees, flowers, birds, stars, clouds, and bodies of water, all of which comprise God's universe. In the launch of Christ's earthly ministry, He selected an array of personalities including rough, boisterous fishermen, a devious tax collector, a detail-inclined physician and characters of various dispositions. This, I believe, was absolutely intentional. It is almost humorous to consider that the forerunner of Christ was a wild man, preaching repentance, wearing a camel-hair cloak and a leather girdle, and whose diet consisted of locusts and wild honey! (Matthew 3:4) Talk about expressive!

Even on the Day of Pentecost (Acts 2), where all of the people had the same mind and purpose, there were seventeen cultures represented. I promise you there may have been conformity to doctrine, but there was not conformity as to culture, neither should there have been. Is it needful for one to entirely lose his personal uniqueness in order to be conformed to the will of God? The answer is obvious.

For too long, too many have tried to confine the Kingdom to those who conformed exclusively to a crew cut and navy knits! It is my opinion that the human expression, i.e., how you comb your hair, what colors you like to wear and the kind of car you drive, is your contribution to diversity and represents the very expression of God Himself. Every culture in the world is part of the creative collage, including the American culture. Your expression is His expression! Dr. Ed Young stated, "We should not fight the culture, but allow culture to be the wind in our (the Church's) sails!"

Why should the Kingdom not be a cross-section representation of all humanity? When we are saved, we lose our old identity with sin, but we never cease to be the "...fearfully and wonderfully made" creature God intended. There should be business executives, blue collar workers, the artistic type, cowboys, those who with special needs, medical professionals, jocks, salesmen, factory workers, 'techno wizards' and every other profession, ethnicity and culture represented in the Kingdom. Jesus Christ died for "...whosoever will," did He not? If so, then you are free to be yourself and we had best toss the cookie-cutter!

32

BEGIN WITH THE END IN VIEW

The red, neon sign flickered its brilliant message, 'Return Rentals,' through the darkness of a snowy January night. A steady line of cars turning in at the same gate let me know this was the right place. After flying into St. Louis for a meeting, it was time to return the compact rental car I had used during my stay.

When I rented the vehicle, there was an agreement signed, stating that I would be the sole driver and that I would be responsible to return the car at the agreed upon time and that it would be returned in the same condition as it was when I picked it up. The final thing was an agreement to be responsible for any damages.

As we begin the New Year, perhaps we would all do well to approach it as we do a rental car, knowing we are responsible for everything we do. In Luke 14:28, Jesus asked an important question to the crowd. "Suppose one of you wants to build a tower. Will he not first sit down and estimate the cost to see if he has enough money to complete it?" In other words, one has to begin with the end in view. Too many people bumble their way through life with no plan or understanding of their accountability at the end of the road.

Friend, we all will one day give an account to God for the vehicle, or life, God loaned to us. Realize your life is not yours, it is a loaner. Recently, I corrected my son at the dinner table because he asked if he could 'borrow' the salt. I replied, "No, you cannot borrow it, but you can have it." If something is borrowed, it is expected to be returned. I know when that salt goes on my son's food, it will be assimilated into his body and will never be returned. But when it comes to our lives, each one of us is merely on loan from God. This is why Paul said, "You are not your own, you were bought with a price. Therefore, honor God with your body."

I have concerns about those who deface God's property, either inwardly or outwardly. Should someone not tell them they are messing with something that does not belong to them? To introduce cell-destroying agents into the bloodstream is counter to the stewardship and custodial oversight with which God entrusted man. The Bible is a manual on moderation. Anything that crosses that line, borders on destruction of private property. Conversely, I am certain God is pleased with anything we do to enhance the property, becoming more health conscious and enlarging our scope of education.

At the end of the trip, the car had to be returned to the place I picked it up. So it is with our lives. When we reach the end, whether the mileage is high or low, the vehicle is returned to God. Ecclesiastes 12:7, "Then shall the dust return to the earth as it was and the spirit shall return unto God who gave it."

Sure enough, when I pulled into the return lot, an attendant met me with a clip board in hand. It was time for the inspection. He walked around the car, looking for dents or scrapes, then opened the trunk and finally inspected the interior. Passing the inspection, I was allowed to go on my way. Rest assured, our lives will be inspected at the end of all things. Every deed, both good and bad; every word, both idle and constructive; every thought, both to build or destroy, will be accounted for. I want, above all things, to pass the final inspection.

There is one final requirement and that is to return the car full of fuel. "Be filled with the Spirit!" is the admonition of Ephesians 5:18. These are the requirements necessary to return the rental without penalty.

Years ago, I walked through an old cemetery in Houston, Texas, reading the epitaphs as I went. One caught my attention that read, "When the Judge of the Ages comes to call your name, it matters not if you won or lost, but how you played the game." Truly, whether we win fame or fortune in this life is not the important thing. It is how you played the game of life. Be careful! Begin with the end in view, knowing we will check back into the place we began.

33

THE 'INTELLIGENT DESIGNER' IS GOD

Often the attack on essential, biblical truth is veiled in half truths. When it comes to foundational beliefs of Christianity, we must become guardians. By foundational beliefs, I am referring to the divine creation, biblical accuracy, the virgin birth, Christ's death, burial and resurrection, etc. These truths are under attack and the front lines have migrated from the distant, left-wing individualists, to the courtrooms of our beloved nation.

Traveling recently, I found myself seated next to a young man from England. He was very pleasant, but also extremely schooled in his arguments against creationism and the existence of God. The need to revisit the basis of Christianity and the desire to teach those principles to my children were re-awakened. Foundational questions must be answered: Is there a God and if so, how do we know? After all, our entire lives are built around all that we either believe or disbelieve. Humanistic thinkers have spoken their liberal opinions loud and clear, 'God is anything you want to worship…including inanimate objects, human beings or your own self, if that is most convenient.'

There is an origination factor to everything. The belief system of every person has a reference point of beginning. For example, if you follow the teaching of an atheistic philosopher, then that is your point of beginning. But then you must trace your philosopher's point of doctrinal origin. Most usually, when you find the 'tap root' of your source, it will wind up beginning in the godless mind of Mr. Darwin and his theory of evolution or some other atheist. The Christian is required to do the same thing. We all would do well to attempt to understand why we believe what we believe. It is not good enough to succumb to a particular way of thinking just because Grandma did it this way. Let us continue back to the root of all we believe. Hopefully, you can authenticate your understanding clearly and contextually within the pages of the Holy Bible.

Being fair, it is incumbent upon believers to ask themselves, "Why do I use the Bible as my reference for time and eternity, instead of a book from one of the thousands of other philosophic minds?" The young man on the airplane posed this very question. Why is the Bible of any more significant than the writing of Plato, Confucius, Aristotle or Darwin? Here are some abbreviated answers as to why I believe the biblical account, and thus believe in God, creation, salvation, etc.

1. The Writers: We are not considering the work of one man. The Bible is a cumulative work of many writers, separated by hundreds, even thousands of years. They did not compare notes, yet their writings dovetail together, confirming one another and perfectly complementing one another. The chances of this occurring by mere fortune are too high to calculate. Fact is, there is but one Author,

the Holy Spirit, working through men. (2 Peter 1:21)

2.   Prophecy: The Old Testament prophets wrote concerning events of which they knew nothing about, yet they came to pass just as they were written. Consider the prophecies of Jesus alone. The prophets foretold His birth and the exact location of it. They wrote of His death and exactly how it would occur, including the fact that not a single bone would be broken. Despite the 17th Century claims of the Muslim Koran that Jesus merely swooned on the cross and then fled to India, historical evidences prove it happened just as it was foretold and witnessed in the Bible. Many other prophecies revolving around the final outcome of battles and cities were proven correct over and over again.

3.   The Intelligent Design: Why do men find it so difficult to give credit where credit is due? Yes, the design of all things is intelligent. The first sentence in the Bible is the explanation. "In the beginning God created…" There is no need to spend one's life attempting to disprove that which is blatantly apparent truth. How did we become part of a galaxy that rotates in perfect harmony with our earth, close enough to the sun to keep us warm, but far enough away to prevent burning us to death? How did we come to have seasons and water cycles and life cycles and the intricate systems of the

human body and…you get the point. The Bible plainly told mankind the earth was round whilst men fearfully voyaged the ocean, hoping they would not fall off the face of the supposed flat planet. So much for human predictions.

4. Archeology: The ruins of biblical cities and events have been thoroughly documented. Finding the ancient Dead Sea Scrolls was a huge discredit to those who purported the Bible to be a modern concoction.

5. Holes in anti-scriptural theory: Those attempting to disprove the Bible with timeline disparities have run into trouble. First, if the earth were billions and billions of years old, we would be knee deep in measurable, cosmic dust that consistently accumulates on our planet. Next, carbon dating has been proven erratic and unreliable. Tests on modern artifacts have shown them to be thousands of years old. Finally, if we were animals that evolved, why did the evolution suddenly stop? If we came from monkeys, why do we not see some part-monkey/part-man hopping around? And, where is the next phase? Why do we not see a part-man/part-flying humanoid attempting his first lift off?

6. Results: The greatest evidence of all is to see those who follow the rules and training of the Bible. When drug addicts repent and are delivered from

their addiction immediately, how do you refute that? Positive thinking, will power, yeah right! We know God exists because we can feel Him and experience Him. (Romans 1:20)

I hope you will become a defender against those who would corrupt the minds of the next generation. There is one, Almighty God, who has a blueprint for each life to follow. To neglect Him is to forsake the only Intelligent Designer.

34

THE DEVIL IN THE DETAILS

"The devil is in the details!" My friend, Jim, states this truth convincingly, and well he should, because his job revolves around the intricate task of managing a large budget. He knows the smallest error in calculation may add up to big trouble when reconciling the account. Most everyone has or will have the task of discovering the most troublesome, difficult times of our lives are more often with the little things of life than the big ones.

Why does the trouble, the complexities or, as Jim puts it, the 'devil,' lay squarely in the middle of details? For one thing, the details are so easily overlooked. It is very easy to see the big picture and even get folks to rally around a large task or grand idea, but working through the endless veins of minutia required to meet the desired goal is where the sweat breaks out. Every man just 'loves' it when his wife buys one of those 'assembly required' gifts. To the buyer, it is very easy to see the completed item on the full-color picture attached to the box. However, more than one bad word has had to be restrained when the job is almost completed, two fingernails are purple, a bloody band-aid is attached to a knuckle and it becomes obvious there are going to be parts left over. What is worse is when the thing on the living room floor bears scarce resemblance to the thing on the cardboard picture. Besides, who can read instructions written in a foreign language anyway? Yes, the devil is in the details.

I read of a wealthy woman who was traveling overseas and saw a bracelet she thought was irresistible so she sent her husband a cable: "Have found wonderful bracelet. Price $75,000. May I buy it?" Her husband promptly wired back this response: "No, price too high." But the cable operator omitted the comma so the woman received the message: "No price too high." She bought the bracelet. What a difference a little comma made!

Great successes are made up of attention to the little things. If you have ever built a house, you can expect it to cost ten percent more than you planned and take ten percent longer than you thought it would. The reason? Details! So it is with raising children, except there are no instructions to go with them when they are taken home from the hospital. If all the details of raising a child were disclosed beforehand, perhaps the human race would become extinct. Had you only known of all the extra trips, practices, late nights, meals on the run, talks on social behavior, manners, spills on the car seat, money, money, money, etc. Guess what? These little extras in life are the very things that determine whether our children will be successful or not. Marriage is the same. Being willing to give above and beyond what you think is right or obligatory are details that lead to success.

The Bible pays close attention to detail. Have you ever been bored when reading historical genealogies in scripture? Remember, so and so begat so and so, who begat so and so, who begat so and so? By this, God allowed us to keep record of tribal and family lineages, even the lineage of Jesus Christ! It required details to do so. We are told in Proverbs to "...despise not the day of small things," reminding us that little things matter. According to Song of Solomon 2:15, "...the little foxes spoil the vine."

Harm can come to any soul via the seemingly insignificant. Failure occurs when we either admit error into our lives or we omit good from our lives. In either case, a little dab will do.

"A little leaven ferments the whole lump of dough." (I Corinthians 5:6) I recall the story of a man who attempted to build a castle overlooking the ocean. He made one grave mistake by mixing his mortar with salt water. In time, the salt in the mortar caused the man's castle to crumble to the ground. The ruins are known to tourists as "The Fool's Castle." All of the man's noble effort was worthless! One detail sealed his fate.

The devil is not the only one interested in details. Our heavenly Father is also. He cares for the sparrow that falls. He waters the flowers no human will ever see. John R. Rice said, "God cares about details. If you comb out some hairs in the morning, the record in heaven is changed." Dream big, but pay close attention to the details. If you do not include God in them intentionally, the little foxes will get more than their share.

35

SHOWDOWN IN SELFVILLE

A weathered, old signboard spanned the entire distance across the narrow, dusty street creating a natural frame for the picturesque, western town into which I was riding. The sign was held up on each end by giant beams that must have taken ten men to pull with a rope, into an upright position. Overhead a smaller pole, from which the sign hung, sagged a bit in the middle. Swinging in the hot breeze, the sign made a rhythmic squeaking sound, to either welcome or bid farewell to all who entered. A scrawny, red hound walked stiff-legged across the street stretching out in the cool shade of the boardwalk for a midday nap. A half dozen horses dozed in the warm sun, still tied to various hitching posts dotting the edge of the street. Sweat dripped from a pair of red mules, making muddy splotches in the dust beneath. They were still hitched to a wagon loaded with trade goods from another location. It was plain to see by the hum of activity this was a lively city. Moving a little closer and shading my eyes against the sun, I read the sign across the entrance of the town, "Welcome to Selfville, Honorable M. Conscious, Sheriff."

My dusty clothes, sweat-stained hat and boots, run-over at the heels, belied my otherwise domesticated style. I was a drifter. Anybody with one eye and a thimble-full of good sense could see by looking, I was the real deal. Dealing on the rough side was my lot. I had survived hand-to-mouth, not caring where I hung my hat, whether jail cell or livery stable. The scar across my cheekbone told a story that the callouses on my hands, especially when doubled into an iron knot, confirmed. Numerous notches on my gun handle were tell-tale signs of a reality I was proud of.

I am known in these parts as Anthony N. Gry. Inside my collar is a pulse pounding louder than a clanking windmill in a tornado. I have come to Selfville on a mission. This, like other missions, would not take long. I'll go to the 'Watering Hole,' have a drink, inquire about the feller I am after and then take care of business. The business would be the fun part. I had already decided how I would lasso his mangy hide from my horse, drag him down the street by his heels, not stopping 'til I got him out of town. Next, I'd cut him loose, bust his chops and see how many teeth I could pull with my bare knuckles. Whatever was left of him would be pushed into the canyon for the coyotes to enjoy.

The same plan had worked elsewhere, why not here? I was almost to the bat-winged doors of the Watering Hole when I caught a motion out of the corner of my left eye. First I thought it was a blowing tumbleweed, and then I recognized it to be the silhouette of a man stepping out from a door across the street. As he closed the door, I read the sign on the window, "Sheriff's Office." Sunlight glinting off his badge let me know this was indeed the law and order of Selfville. Oddly, he wasn't wearing a gun. His steady walk, defined by the jingle of his spurs, made an interesting cadence. Before he made it over, I had already studied him, and I knew him before I had ever met him. I secretly had hoped I would not have to shoot him too. I was about to discover what I was up against.

"Howdy," the old gentleman said in a rough voice. "Right back to you," I replied, keeping the brim of my hat low over my eyes. "What brings you here, stranger, and what's your name?" he asked. If he was going to be that forward with me then I would return the favor. In slow phrases, I said, "I am Anthony N. Gry, my friends call me Angry for short. I am here to rearrange some dental work for a fellow, maybe more."

Just then the sheriff walked up real close. His kind old eyes squinted to narrow slits and it seemed you could see a little fire in them. "Sonny," he said, "You'd best find a hos' and ride out." Tufts of white hair were blowing gently from beneath his tall Stetson. "You'd better heed my warnin'! I have seen better gunslingers than you go down in a heap. Besides, we have only one law here in Selfville and there ain't no tolerance!"

"Oh yeah? What is your one measly law?" I retorted, unamused. I shall never forget his words. Must have been the tears welling up in his eyes that burned the moment into my brain forever. He stammered in a soft voice, "It is the law of kindness…lovin' yore neighbor as much as you care about yourself."

I was speechless. Here I am, ol' Angry himself, the biggest pistol-packin', fire-breathin', trouble makin' dude with the biggest two fists full of hades you ever saw. I was just looking for trouble! Suddenly the little old sheriff of Selfville shuts me down with one simple law. He was not finished with his speech either.

"Son, we instituted this law about 20 years ago when a gentleman came in here and revolutionized this once lawless, drunken town. I don't recall his name just yet, but he was so kind and he carried some amazing scars in his hands. Looked as if he had seen a battle or two hisself. He told us we could get rid of the hundreds of laws in our old law book. Before that, it seems the judge had to write a new law every day to cover the loophole in the last one. The more laws we had, the more outlaws we had. We could not keep up with all of them anyway. The man said if we could maintain one overriding law, we could make kindling out of our law book. So, we did. Sonny boy, that was the best move we ever made. Since then we have hardly had to take anyone out to boot hill."

Now I could see this was getting really serious. The old man pressed in even closer. I could smell the onions on his breath when he said these final words, "Mister, my name is Sheriff Conscious and I am going to have to ask you to get rid of that hog-leg on your hip or leave town." With that, he reached over and gently lifted my six-shooter from its holster. I started to resist, but found that I could not. "Now, you can either leave this with me and live by the law, or else you best be out of town by dark."

I stumbled to the Watering Hole and found a corner chair.
A friendly lady politely asked, "What'll it be partner? Root
beer or iced tea?" I don't remember what I said. All I
know is when I saw the hand-painted sign over the bar that
said, "Do unto others as you would have them do unto
you," I got real sick, like how I feel after a three-day drunk.
Next thing I knew, it was dark and I was still walking away
from Selfville. I was without food, without my horse,
without my gun and certainly without my pride. But I'll be
whipped if I was going back to face that sheriff again. That
was the last time yours truly, Old Angry, ever went back to
Selfville. I heard the signboard creak one last time as if to
say, "Good Riddance."

36

STOP TREATING SYMPTOMS AND FIX THE ROOT CAUSE

When beset with a headache, a backache or any other ache of the human body we, like most Americans, run for the medicine cabinet in search of some type of pain relief. We fail to realize pain is the body's way of sending a signal that all is not well with a particular area of the body.

Rather than concentrating on fixing the source of the problem, we simply attempt to pacify and alleviate the symptoms, or pain, of what is wrong. This phenomenon is also true in our emotional lives, in relationships and in our spiritual lives as well. While the liquor, gambling, work and adrenaline hide the pain for a while, the actual ailment may be getting worse.

Passing by a small, rural home recently, I could not help contrasting the difference in lifestyles from our modern, urban life as compared to the rural homesteads of almost a century ago. The differences are vast. It is right to ponder whether or not our modern inventions and conveniences have actually made the human family better over the long run. We are conditioned to think bigger and faster is better, and he with the most 'toys' is the winner. Not necessarily so!

Our wants and our competitive nature create a vacuum requiring longer work hours, or two, three and four jobs, or whatever it takes until we are stretched thin. Put on top of that the very subtle and unstated pressure that says, "If your kids aren't enrolled in three sports, if your kids aren't wearing the latest fashions, have the newest games, belong to such and such camp, if they aren't riding in an SUV, then you are failing as a parent." Soon, we fall into a rat race of multiple jobs, schedules and sporting events, not to mention the maximized need for more maintenance on the car, the house, the yard, etc. You can see how this can get out of control rather quickly. It is a good thing God gave only 24 hours in a day or we may have all died from exhaustion by now.

Contrast that with the farm scene of a few years ago. People were content to raise their families, even large families, in small, frame homes. There was simple gratefulness to have a home and not a competition to outdo the Joneses. Families did chores together, chores which were vital to their existence and not merely a means of giving a kid a large allowance. Free time for children was spent using their imagination, playing along the creek, building forts and riding horses. Today our children appear weak and anemic when it comes to many skills beyond watching movies and playing video games.

It was a time when the major influencers of children were their parents. Boys helped their dads in the field and learned to work with their hands, while girls learned to sew, cook and can vegetables alongside their mothers. Schools were not continually chipping away at parental influence with longer school days and shorter summer breaks. It was about family, about co-existing peacefully. An old maxim out of New England was quoted by Calvin Coolidge: "Eat it up, wear it out, make it do and do without." Contained in this sentence is a wealth of information, lived out by our forefathers. Our children would do well to learn these values today.

So, what do we do? We cannot go back to pre-modern America. We have to deal with what is given us. What is the answer to the ulcers, the anti-depressants and the pain killers that are doing nothing for the real problem? Somehow, we need the grace of God to help us learn to treat the source of the symptom and not the symptom itself. We do this by learning to say no to extra obligations, to peer pressure at every age and by living in terms which make inner peace more valuable than any 'thing' one can purchase at the supermarket. One of the greatest treatments for an ailing soul is to be satisfied with one's status in life. I am not inferring we should ever stop learning and growing spiritually, but if our efforts to achieve become counter-productive to the big picture, what are we really gaining? I have preached too many funerals of young people with big dreams and funerals of thirty-somethings who thought they would someday clasp the 'dangling carrot' just ahead of them. When will we stop looking for that fictitious pot of gold at the end of the rainbow? Perhaps it is time to take Jesus' advice: Be content with food, shelter and clothing. These things He promised to provide for His own. After that, it is up to us. We can either embark on a simple, peace-filled walk with Him or we can join the rat race of modernism. When you cross life's finish line, you will leave all the stuff behind. What really counts is whether or not you made the time to get to know Jesus Christ through His Word. Now, pour another cup of coffee and make a list of ways you can simplify your life. Unload your basket and get into the express lane. You have been treating symptoms long enough!

37

A LITTLE RED WAGON IN A HOSPITAL

My curiosity got the best of me. There was no way I could keep from looking into the little red wagon being pulled down the hallway of a hospital. The lady pulling the wagon was upbeat and smiling as she made her way through the constant stream of people.

Inside the wagon was on of the most heart-rending sights I have ever witnessed. She was probably in her middle 20's. Both of her hands and her feet were crippled and deformed. She wore a bulky brace about her neck. Propped on a pillow, the only things that appeared to move with any coordination were her eyes. They were alive and in some odd way, smiling.

A few minutes later I wound up in the cafeteria where this amazing tandem was in line for food. It was then I noticed the girl in the wagon could not speak nor hear. Her caregiver was communicating with her by hand signals. In the lunch room, every bite of food was carefully placed at the girl's mouth. When the caregiver got up to retrieve some napkins, she walked directly by my table. On her way back, I stopped her and commended her for such wonderful care and the kindness with which she appeared to give it. I will never forget her words to me, "It is my privilege…she is my sister!"

For some reason my food was not as enjoyable that day, especially when considering how prone I am, and I assume we all are, to whining about the little things in life we do not possess. This phenomenon is true at every level of wealth. We all want more, bigger, better, etc. When you look from the perspective of that little red wagon, life is really good for us all.

There is a disease among us. It is called discontentment. We are dis-eased because we never seem to find a place of acceptance and ease with whatever place we may be in life. This is not a suggestion that we all should never try to improve ourselves, but it is merely an attempt to help us see what we have and curb our tendency to always look across the fence.

I found a verse in the Bible that deserves a second look regarding this subject. Proverbs 30:15-16 speaks of a horseleech. I assume this is a particular variety of those slick, slimy, blood-sucking, water-bound creatures. By nature, they never get enough to eat. Their entire mentality is defined in one word, give. By give, they really mean take. Life is all about themselves and what they can secure from someone else.

This scripture also describes other takers in the world. The common denominator is they are never satisfied. These scriptural illustrations are: the grave, the barren womb, the earth that is not filled with water, and fire.

You will never see a sign above a cemetery saying, "We want your business!" As long as time stands, there will be a need for cemeteries. The grave is never full.

You will never hear a woman who was unable to have a child say, "I am over it. I really am glad I didn't have any kids. I did not want the experience anyway!" Never! As long as she is alive, there will always be the yearning regret of never having children.

The earth never says, "Okay, enough water!" As long as the sun, through evaporation, lifts vapors from the planet, there will be an insatiable thirst for water.

And fire – you will never see a house fire suddenly go out all by itself, midway through the burn, saying, "That is enough. Let us leave the rest." A thousand times no! It will burn everything it can consume and then try to get the trees, the hay meadow, the barn and anything else consumable. Human beings can fall into the same category.

My prayer is that we all can realize just how rich we are. To a starving man, a crumb of bread makes one rich. I have found our blessings are more easily viewed from the position of humility. As members of the land of the free, we struggle with that perspective. How long has it been since you have counted the blessings God has given you, many of which are of inestimable value and cannot be computed in dollars and cents? A view from a wagon in a hospital helped me understand a most important fact. Blessings are relative in nature.

38

GRACE FROM A TURTLE'S PERSPECTIVE

Springtime fishing is one of my favorite things to do. While taking in the scenic beauty of the water, trees and even a few fish with my wife, a most unusual event occurred. We found a stranded turtle. I am talking really stranded! At the base of one of the giant, overhanging cliffs on Beaver Lake, with sheer, rock walls going straight up some 80 or 90 feet, was a poor, little turtle clinging to life on a tiny slab of rock. We would not have given it a second look, until we saw that his shell was cracked. It was then we noticed the little guy was not a water-type turtle. He was a land rover, a terrapin. This spelled trouble.

Soon, we put the puzzle together. By some misfortune, the turtle had fallen from the top of the cliff above, thus the broken shell. Somehow he had been lucky enough to grasp on to this small piece of rock, just in time to save his life. Remember, terrapins do not swim!

Realizing the distress of the animal, we turned the boat back for a closer look. The predicament of the turtle was huge, and the possibility of its survival was zero. It was as good as dead. Sharp eyes, nimble feet, and a carry-along shelter would not be enough to help this fellow survive against the odds it was facing. He was trapped by a 90-foot wall in front and a half mile wide lake behind him. His would be a slow, fear-filled death. It was a picture of absolute doom, of fear, of complete peril. It was a picture of you and me.

We have counselors that can help untangle many emotional webs. Medical doctors can evaluate and prescribe medications that alleviate most physical ailments. Books can make you wise. True friends can bring solace to your hurting heart. Music may relax you for a few minutes. Pleasure is only for a season. When it comes to the issue of our sinfulness, we are as helpless as the poor turtle.

Scripture declares, "All have sinned!" (Romans 3:23) That means me, that means you – all of us have come short of God's intention and purpose. We then understand the awful peril we face. On one side, the cliff of sin separates us from what we should have been. On the other side, the waters of death and eternal damnation lap at our very souls. We are trapped! If left to ourselves, we will surely die.

Some believe their keen abilities will save them. Modern Pharisees believe that if they embrace enough laws, they can make it. The philanthropist hopes he can escape by giving away his fortunes. Do-gooders assume God will save them for all the kind deeds they have done. Truth is, only the sacrifice of our Lord Jesus has the ability to save you and me from our sins.

It was a good feeling to lift the turtle from its watery demise and into the safety of the boat. We took the crawling critter straight across the lake and set him free on the shore. If turtles can smile, this one had an ear-to-ear going on! This is grace, unmerited favor, from a turtle's point of view.

The only way you and I will ever land safely on the sunny shores of sweet deliverance will be by the help and grace of God Almighty. He made a way, the only way, through His eternal plan to save mankind. When we submit our lives, becoming obedient to His plan, we can feel His hand lift us from our low estate of doom and into the boat of salvation.

Pastor Don Johnson wrote a song entitled, "God's Hand Reached Further Down than I Could Reach Up." The cross is God's rescue boat for all the trapped turtles. Give Him your life today!

EPILOGUE

We may never know the value of words. A simple sentence can unleash the atrocities of war, or provide an unmistakable pathway to peace. A few words in a letter released President Nixon from his position and duties. Abraham Lincoln's ten-sentence address at Gettysburg remains an immortal legacy to the power of script.

Oh the power of words! The writer of Proverbs said, "A word fitly spoken is like apples of gold in pitchers of silver." While I have never owned one of those, I understand the writer was inferring their beauty and ability to create ambiance, in space and in mind. Words can be beautiful and lasting. We all long for such accommodations in our own souls. With words we are affirmed or broken. As such, great care must be given to how we use them.

Too often I have seen the life work of great men and women buried with them, their stories and experiences, their victories and failures, and more. This loss is too great for words. The sharing of one story could save pain for generations. Without writing, words and stories, like the fog, dissipate with time.

Beliefs put in writing become fair game for scrutiny and reveal the truest convictions of the soul. Many state their beliefs in a closed environment, but will never put their thoughts up for the investigation of higher thinking.

Only through writing will one's thoughts and legacy be truly preserved. By putting thoughts to paper we have the ability to look deeply into, and wrestle with, the true meanings of all our Creator intended. Words on paper are treasures from centuries ago; landmarks against which we may buoy our own beliefs as we play our short role on life's grand stage.

I look forward to sharing more in the future and from hearing your point of view as well. Let me inspire you to write, as others have done for me.

Tim S. Estes

Made in the USA
Monee, IL
12 February 2020